Advance Praise for Jes Baker and *Landwhale*

"It's tempting to call Jes Baker 'fearless,' but to do so would diminish her profound capacity for vulnerability and, by extension, her strength. The thing that makes Jes such a force is that she is so brave, so funny, so blazing, so herself, even in the face of fear. I do not know what we would do without her."

—Lindy West, *New York Times* bestselling author of *Shrill*

"Funny, kind, wise, generous, and incredibly real—Jes Baker's writing will have you feeling seen, heard, and held. I enjoyed every minute of reading this book, even when it made me cry. Instead of calling to us from a finish line that seems impossibly far away, Jes shares a path to self-love that she's still on with us. And in her story we can find the joy in the journey itself, even if we can't yet see the destination."

—Ijeoma Oluo, *New York Times* bestselling author of *So You Want To Talk About Race*

"With the perfect tidal wave of humor and candid emotion, Jes once again shows me how to not only love my own body, but every body around me, as well. It's as if she's written *Landwhale* about the daily complicated love affair I have in my skin, and I'll never stop reading it. All women, at all stages of their journey, must read this book!"

—Brittany Gibbons, *New York Times* bestselling author of *Fat Girl Walking* and *The Clothes Make the Girl (Look Fat)?*

"In *Landwhale*, Jes Baker asks the hard questions of herself and of our fat-hating culture, and she never sugarcoats the answers. Her memoir is full of humor and grace and honesty. She treats the reader like a friend, and on every page she sends the message: *You're not alone.*"

—Sarai Walker, author of *Dietland*

"Jes Baker's words are ointment for the soul. I want to give this book to every person who's ever struggled with their body and its place in this world. Read this book. Thank me later."

—Julie Murphy, #1 *New York Times*
bestselling author of *Dumplin'*

LANDWHALE

LANDWHALE

On Turning Insults Into Nicknames,
Why Body Image Is Hard, and
How Diets Can Kiss My Ass

JES BAKER

SEAL PRESS

Seal Press
Hachette Book Group
1290 Avenue of the Americas, New York, NY 10104
www.sealpress.com
@SealPress

Printed in the United States of America
First Edition: May 2018

Published by Seal Press, an imprint of Perseus Books, LLC, a subsidiary of Hachette Book Group, Inc. The Seal Press name and logo is a trademark of the Hachette Book Group.

The publisher is not responsible for websites (or their content) that are not owned by the publisher.

Lesley Kinzel quote used with permission.

Portion of Kim Selling poem used with permission. "Fat Bottomed Girls" originally performed in 2011.

Print book interior design by Jeff Williams.

Library of Congress Cataloging-in-Publication Data has been applied for.

ISBNs: 978-1-58005-681-6 (paperback), 978-1-58005-682-3 (e-book)

LSC-C

10 9 8 7 6 5 4 3 2 1

We have tried to prove to the thin world that we are worthy for far too long.

If you are going to be brave, be brave for the fat people.

—IJEOMA OLUO

Contents

Trigger Warnings, Disclaimers, and Other Things

HEY, FRIEND!

When I asked a few brilliant minds to read selected sections from this book and send back their critiques, many left comments in the margins that went a lot like: "*Holy shit*, maybe consider giving people a heads-up that there is some rough stuff in here so they don't pass out mid-chapter, okay?" That, combined with the fact that I cried all over my keyboard while typing half of this memoir, convinced me that a *Hey, I'm writing about real life, and real life can occasionally be difficult, so please be gentle with your heart while flipping through these pages* was in order.[1]

So, in the spirit of transparency, I offer you this insider tip: The book you're holding? It's basically one long-ass trigger.

....

1. I'm astounded that my keyboard still works after endless months of salty eyeball flooding. Hewlett Packard, keep up the good work.

Tough topics covered that you might want to mentally buckle up for:

Self-hatred
Eating disorders
Weight-loss surgery
Bedbugs (I'm *still* trying to emotionally recover)
Fatphobia
Embarrassing personal failure
Diet-ey diet talk about *a lot of* diets

I wrote *Landwhale* for three reasons: 1) I wanted to give these stories a permanent home; 2) I wanted to offer my personal narrative to you in the hope that you might feel a little less alone after turning the last page; and 3) the title was too good to *not* be on a book cover.

With any luck, you'll find some validation, solidarity, and humor within these pages as well.

I will also disclose that some names have been changed, not because I believe that divulging every last detail is a sin, but because many other people in this universe do.

You're holding a story. It's a sad one. A scary one. A common one. A happy one. A tragic one. A privileged one. An *impossible-to-properly-articulate* one. A relatable one. An unwelcome one. A lucky one. An alienating one. A confusing one. A brave one. A safe one. A problematic one. An unfinished one. A true one.

It is all of these things, but, simply put, it is mine.

All of that said, welcome! I'm glad you're here. So hold on to those britches of yours, because we're about to talk about some really important shit.

Holding your hand (consensually, of course) as we dive in,

CHAPTER 1

....

This Was All Just a Big Mistake

I AM AN *impressively* terrible businesswoman.

I became "Jes, The Militant Baker: conspicuous fat chick, beauty-myth challenger, shit talker, petty blocker, Twitter amateur, and internet human with more followers than any person from Tucson deserves" by complete accident. The fact that you're holding this book in your hands right now? Total fluke. In fact, I keep expecting someone important who is in charge of something big (Google? Amazon maybe? Even Kmart would do) to come out and say, "Sorry guys, this was all just one big mistake! Jes, delete everything you've written online. Everyone else, carry on."

I'm still not ruling that out.

So, no. I never imagined, back when I started typing center-justified blog posts (I still have serious internet shame around this) on a shoddily designed Blogger site—first about vintage kitchenware *yawn* and then about my plus-size body—that it would lead to this. "This" being becoming a somewhat well-known fat person on the internet whom thousands of people praise and *even more* people pray an untimely death for. "This" being a future containing invitations to participate in documentaries, film corporate campaigns and offers to write Upworthy articles (which no doubt require hours of editing on their end). "This" being a creepily detailed Wikipedia page about my past written by strangers, a delightfully scathing shout-out on Breitbart, the chance to lecture at universities about why being nice is a *really good thing*, and the opportunity to be in the same room as (and the inexplicable privilege to be ignored by) the accomplished actress Danielle Brooks. When I started writing online, none of this crossed my baby blogger mind.

I just wanted a couple dozen people (honestly, I would have settled for five—friends included) to read my hastily typed fat-girl feels and the opportunity to take lots of pictures of myself using my DLSR, which I fondly named Midge. I was bored by my deteriorating relationship and needed a hobby because watching *River Monster* marathons every single night with a lifeless partner who only liked eating chicken nuggets, wearing Tapout shorts, and refusing to let me drive just wasn't doing it for me anymore.

So, I sat on my bed, opened my computer, shoved an SD card into my camera, and started blogging for no other reason than to distract myself from the toothy perils that apparently lurk in every body of water (also: is Jeremy Wade *even his real name?* As the host of a show filmed in bodies of water, it just . . . seems awfully convenient) and a person who would rather stare blankly at a screen than interact with another human. Especially me.

Oh, the *glamour*. Oh, *the life*.

And somehow, five years later . . . here I am: two books published, innumerable conference and college lectures given, and hundreds of thousands of followers who have formed an incredible community and have taught me more about body politics, fat empowerment, and mental health than I could have ever imagined. I'm still hastily typing and taking lots of pictures, but now I am both existing and producing content under a shockingly hot spotlight that comes with the un-ditchable (trust me, I've tried) requirement of being what some adults like to call a *businesswoman*. That's what they call someone who identifies as a lady person and makes some money doing things on their own when they're a grown-up, right?

If so, I suppose that's what I am, like it or not.

And the reality is that I suck at all of it.

I'll own that the success is both startling and exciting. A large part of my visibility can be attributed to my dedication to authenticity, challenging social norms, bad jokes, critical thinking in a world that prefers the easy way out, as well as undeniable privilege and sheer luck. I'm pretty great at continuing to excel in all of these things. The business part though? Not so much.

I'm not aiming for self-deprecation. I'm simply stating a fact—one that is well known by any volunteer who has helped me run a "successful" (to others, anyway; it was a clusterfuck behind the scenes) five-hundred-person conference when I had no idea what a conference should look like or what intersectionality was.[1] You can also poll anyone who has emailed me in the last five years; I would imagine that 87 percent of them would agree with my statement after having waited nine months for a reply. And I'm being generous.

To be fair, though, I do receive anywhere from 21 to 198[2] emails a day, and every single one of them (besides the Blue Apron shipping update that reminds me I forgot to cancel my overpriced subscription *again*) contains something complicated that requires me to either write an essay in reply, link multiple items I've lost on my unorganized desktop, or schedule a Skype-oriented meeting. Given that the thought of having to make a phone call causes a panic attack, the Skype requests consequently leave me in a frenzied state where a benzo seems like the only way through.

....

1. Permission to burn me alive at the Activist Stake granted.

2. Lazy estimate because: terrible businesswoman.

It's stressful AF. That's what I'm trying to say here.

So stressful that it's caused me to get a cold and break out in hives more than I ever broke out in teenage acne.

I solved this problem (though far too late in my career) by creating the best auto-response in the existence of the internet. It goes something like this:

Life is wild, isn't it? Your inbox? Probably even wilder. (Mine, too.) *So: I'm trying a little email-experiment!*

I've rounded up the top 6 topics that most people email me about—and I've answered every single question, just for you! **If your email falls under one of the top 6 topics, consider this note your official response.** (Ta da! I'm throwing handfuls of happiness your way!)

If your email pertains to some other topic—or if you're my grandma who's sending me chain emails like it's 1998, my speaking agent, my publisher, in the media, an active client, or, like, the ghost of Kurt Vonnegut—**you'll get a separate response from me as speedily as humanly possible.**

Sending you ALL KINDS of love,

—*Jes*

If you wrote to me because . . .

1. You're wondering where you can find more body-positive resources. You're in luck! I've compiled 340+ awesome links and wrote a book!

2. You'd love to bring me to your campus or event to speak. I'm absolutely honored! I'll respond as soon as I can and will additionally connect you to my speaking agent. He's a peach. (You can find basic info here while you wait for a reply.)

3. You have a question about your business, your writing, or where to find XYZ. I love inquisitive + curious people, but I also love self-reliant people! I recommend using the almighty Google (and your own intuition) to answer your own question because you are so damn smart. And also b/c responding isn't always possible . . . this inbox is bananas. Truth.

4. You've worked on something really amazing and you're wondering if I will share it. I'm SO proud of you! I'm also unable to share everything that comes my way, but keep on kicking ass, my friend!

5. You just want to say "thank you" or share your story. Thank YOU. I think you're amazing and appreciate every note like this that drops into my inbox. Even if I'm not able to respond to every email, just know that your story is honored, safe, and heard. And that I'll put it in my Permanent Happy File so I can keep it + your awesomeness forever. HUGS!

6. You're struggling and really need help. I'm so genuinely sorry you're going through it right now. If you're struggling with **body-image shit,** click (link with body-image pep talk and resources). **If you're in crisis**, click (link with mental health pep talk and resources) or call 1-800-784-2433. I'm rooting for you. You are important to this world, and I'm sending you so much love.

True to form, I just found a typo in a response that has already been sent to hundreds of influential contacts. No big deal.

See? Sure, I run a "business," but I'm an amazing failure at it even when bragging about my best work. I don't know if going back and fixing the typo would defeat my compelling argument that I've just spent twenty paragraphs writing. (Don't count them; that was a sloppy estimate.)

However, this automatic reply has served its purpose. I've yet to catch a cold or break out in email-induced hives since implementing my brilliant riposte. The feedback has consisted of just a few "Your auto-reply is amazing, can I copy it?" (Yes, you can. I didn't come up with something this clever without help) and "It's really effing annoying to get this kick-back every time I email you" responses. I feel you, my friend; getting an email wishing you magic and a wonderful day (with *genuinely* misspelled, for God's sakes) sucks.

Sometimes, I do trudge through the answering of seven thousand emails, though. Eventually, the guilt adds up, the number in bold next to the word "inbox" increases, and the dates that the emails were sent are shoved in my face by Gmail ("Hey, asshole, they sent this three and a half weeks ago. Get your shit together"), and it all becomes impossible to ignore.

On these special occasions, my custom is often to audibly sigh, dig in . . . and skim.

Last year, I opened my inbox and read (just kidding, skimmed) this guy:

Hi Jes!
I'm emailing from Imagination TV in New Zealand.

We are the makers of the TV series called **Name I Skimmed**'s "**Show's name I skimmed**"—a factual travel series about health and beauty around the world. The first series broadcast in 120 countries around the world including cable in the USA, and won a New York Festivals Award.

We are shooting in NYC in August—an episode about the body— and would love to know if you might be interested in talking to us on the programme!

The episode in NYC sees **Skimmed Name** looking at beauty standards and body image. What beauty standards and beauty ideals are at play today? How realistic are these and how have they changed over the past few decades, not just in regards to size wise but also colour, gender, and age? Also, most importantly, how can we learn to accept and love our bodies more no matter what their shape, size, colour, and no matter what the media tells us we should look like. I have included a link to the show below.

Did I click the link? I don't remember.
Things I did remember:

1. NYC.

2. The invitation for this fat girl to discuss her favorite topic: why beauty standards are bullshit.

3. NYC.

I fucking love NYC. I was in.

When the shooting day arrived, it was summer in the city, and I was walking toward the Loeb Boathouse and cursing the fact that the construction inside Central Park had forced my Uber to drop me off several avenues (not streets, *avenues*; there is a lengthy difference) from our lakeside meeting location. Didn't the city planners realize it was 160 degrees, with the same amount of humidity? Probably. But they also probably didn't care. After all, this is the magical city that never sleeps—if you can make it there, you can make it anywhere—that also had mountains of garbage lining every sidewalk and was over capacity with people who would shoulder check you for walking too slow (I've visited enough to become one of those proud shoulder-checking assholes). Being dropped off so far away meant I had to hustle, which didn't bode well with the suffocating humidity, which quickly becomes messy when combined with the amazing amount of sweat I normally produce on a daily basis. The daily amount? Let's just say it's a lot.

Already drenched and barely on time, I met the producer (wiping my hand on my suffocating layered dress—*who wears multiple layers in NYC in the summer? What was I thinking?*—before shaking hers) and waited for our television host. I informed the filming team that I had a rash from an unknown cause on my right arm that I had covered up with foundation, so if they could film from the left, that would be great. I'm sure at that point the makeup had melted off, but they nodded good-naturedly as I internally groaned about how much of a glamorous superstar I continuously failed to be.[3] The host arrived, seemingly twelve feet tall, svelte, with long blonde hair flowing behind her graceful frame, which was dressed effortlessly in white shorts and a knotted chambray top (didn't she know that all chambray clothing highlights sweat? Maybe she didn't sweat?[4]). We greeted each other with another (dress-wiped) handshake. I had too much empathy to force her into a sweaty hug.

"It's so wonderful to meet you!" she grinned. "I have to tell you that I never research who I'm meeting, though. I love to get to know them in person."

To which I replied, "I also have no idea who you are, but I love NYC, and although your producer just said your name, I already forgot it, but you seem like a really nice human."

Yeah, right. I said something about how wonderful that was and how I was thrilled to meet her and thanks for thinking of me for the show.

The next hour was spent on a fucking rowboat in the middle of a goddamn lake with maximum humidity causing me to sweat

....

3. I had visited urgent care a few days before to try to figure out how to make the conspicuous rash disappear and left with a handful of prescriptions to help with the swelling, prescribed by a baffled nurse. I found out months later that it was from a nightmare-inducing infestation of bedbugs. I should have been quarantined, not traveling across the country.

4. She didn't.

so much it looked like I had fallen out and climbed back in. If she needed a single tissue blot I certainly didn't see it, whereas I would have sold my car for anything absorbent (a bath sheet, maybe?) that I could use to wipe my neck.

As we swung our oars the wrong way for sixty minutes, the producers (also not sweating—what sort of genetic anomalies were we dealing with here? Do New Zealanders not have sweat glands?) followed us in another boat, bellowing instructions like "Talk about the fifth graders who hate their bodies!" and "You're going the wrong way again, Jes; try rowing backward!" Somehow, we managed to chat about how harmful it is to idolize one body type.

At one point, she stopped rowing for a moment and somberly confessed, "Sometimes, I wonder how many people I harmed by being visible and part of that idealized demographic." I surveyed her for a moment, with her golden hair slightly moving with the wind (that I certainly didn't feel) and her long and slender arms clutching her stationary paddle.

"Well, perhaps. You are a traditionally attractive person." I stated the obvious nonchalantly while wiping the sweat out of my eyes, trying to say it in a complimentary way. "But this has been going on for centuries and is systemic . . . y'know?" I added desperately in an attempt to not exacerbate her obvious guilt.

After overhearing me beg one of the cameramen for something to tie back my dripping hair with (they had nothing—*nothing*), the producer called the row-boating section a wrap. Whether this decision was made out of a gracious amount of pity or concern for their sweat-covered electrical equipment, I'm still not sure.

It took us an embarrassingly long time to dock the boat in its designated area, but I was relieved to be out of that hellish wooden torture device and on land, where at least I could use my hands to fan myself with the production script while we moved to the center of the park for a few more scenes.

We started filming the "beginning" of the episode, which included her theatrical entrance into Central Park. I watched as they captured the slender host delicately sauntering down the flights of concrete stairs "on her way to meet me," and from the sidelines I couldn't help but notice groups of people stopping and whispering to each other as they took pictures from afar. The Official TV Host Tissue Blotter (unnecessary; also, where was *mine?*) waved them away, and the cameras continued to film as she stopped to fix a bride's dress while a couple was having their picture taken.

"Great!" the producer said. We moved to the fountain for another shot (at this point, I should have realized that they had no compassion for my body's inability to cope with humidity while standing near any water source in hundred-degree heat). "Now, Jes, this is where you are meeting her for the first time. I want both of you to walk toward each other and then greet enthusiastically. And Jes—make sure you start from that corner and hug before you introduce yourself."

I tottered (my chub rub was in full rage mode at this point) over to my designated spot, still drenched, and faced the woman who was already airily striding toward me in a way that made me think that she might be Gwyneth Paltrow's sister. In comparison, I felt like I was capable of only lumbering in her direction, my fat body (the blessed reason I was there) seeming more cumbersome than ever. I kept a smile on my face for the camera, but I'm sure my eyes showed my growing dread about the fact that I had to wrap my salty and sticky body around this unfortunate, elegant woman.

We greeted. We hugged. We took a picture that I was instructed not to share until the episode aired, the filmographers called it a wrap, and then, with a visible air of relief, the crew left.

I too felt relief, wanting nothing more than some goddamn air myself.

I started to walk through the park, wondering why in the hell I had signed up for something like this, and then joined an awestruck crowd that was circled around a man using a rope to completely encompass himself in a six-foot bubble.

I chose a bench next to a young and seemingly charming family with two small children and pulled out my phone to reread the original email and see what I had just participated in.

"Hi Jes!

I'm emailing from Imagination TV in New Zealand.

We are the makers of the TV series *Rachel Hunter's Tour of Beauty*."

Nonplussed and still uncertain about the show I had just filmed, I googled Rachel Hunter.

I am the kind of millennial people write disparaging articles about.

Rachel Hunter: *Actress, supermodel, and ex-wife of Rod Stewart. Has appeared on the front of* Italian Vogue, Elle, Harper's Bazaar, *and twice on the cover of* Sports Illustrated Swimsuit Issue. *Famous for a million reasons and is only unknown by one person in the world: Jes Baker, a sweaty, fat blogger from Arizona who doesn't read her emails.*

I scrolled through images, dumbfounded. Our boat conversation and the unwelcome groups of paparazzi were starting to make more sense. On the one hand, it was pleasant to get to know someone without pretenses. On the other hand, I might have just given Rachel Goddamn Hunter bedbugs.

The toddler next to me projectile vomited all over his parents and, incapable of handling anything else that day, I took it as a sign that it was time to leave.

Lost in thought about my impressive lack of research when it came to the projects I sign up for, I slowly walked back through

Central Park, narrowly missing a bicyclist. He was wearing a helmet but it felt like the both of us barely escaped dramatic deaths. "God, I should wear a helmet when I ride a bike too," I thought as I started to rapidly run through a mental list of things fully functioning adults do that I don't. "Yes. I'm definitely going to buy a helmet," I promised myself. "I'm also going to get that year-long-overdue oil change, return those Amazon packages, and organize the mountain of clothes on my bedroom floor."

"Lord," I thought, as the list continued to grow, "I *really* need to get my shit together."

Of course, I didn't buy a helmet when I got home. I also didn't change my oil, visit UPS, or sort the ninety-two black outfits strewn across the floor of my room. That would have been alarmingly responsible. But I *did* learn perhaps one of the most important lessons to date: a real businesswoman doesn't skim through emails once and say yes.

A real businesswoman skims through at least twice.

CHAPTER 2

6 Ways to Hate Your Body

1) Purchase your first piece of "unflattering" clothing.
Shopping alone as a thirteen-year-old felt like one of my first moments of extravagant independence. While my mom waited on a
bench outside the store, I trotted into Sears; an unsupervised preteen who had a little bit of money and no idea what she was doing.
I quickly assumed the air of a girl who often shopped alone because
of her uncontainable amount of style expertise, and breezily glanced
around, attempting to hide the fact that I had no idea where I was
going until I finally caught a glimpse of the enormous sign labeled
"Women" hanging from the ceiling. I slung my clear vinyl handbag
over my shoulder (told you I was stylish), walked over to where the
sign swayed, and planted myself directly underneath it.

Riffling through the blouses in front of me, I quickly found the
top of my dreams: a light lime-green cotton shirt with elastic-lined
cap sleeves covered in a pattern of miniature white flowers. I purchased it immediately. Proud of my new and very trendy selection, I wore it as often as I could, until a few weeks later when my
mom pulled me aside and suggested that I consider getting rid of it

because it was "unflattering" on my arms. With tears in her eyes as well as mine, she was quick to assure me that it was okay, that someday I would find a man who would love me for me and not for the way I looked. I never wore the shirt again.

2) Worship teen periodicals.

My house didn't believe in magazine subscriptions,[1] so I was left to my own devices when it came to accumulating those beautiful and brightly colored manuals on how to become a paragon of teenage femininity. "My own devices" usually meant slyly sliding a copy of *Seventeen* or *YM* behind a plastic separator on the conveyer belt while my mother checked out at the grocery store. As she arranged the bags of purchased food in the cart, I would quickly slip the cashier a five-dollar bill after she scanned the barcode underneath Josh *Hot-nett's* beautiful face and then tucked the purchase into my bag for later reading. I eventually collected a newsstand-worthy stack of teen style magazines and would pore over them every day, absorbing the tips about how to make your butt look smaller in jeans (answer: enormous pockets), nodding in knowing solidarity at the "Say Anything" advice column where that one girl got earwax on her crush's headphones after borrowing them (sorry, but it's over between the two of you, girl), and tearing out pages of the summer's hottest makeup trends and attaching them to my wall.

What never seemed to be spelled out on the pages but was always evident from looking at my Scotch-taped collages was that the girls who knew and had it all . . . were thin. This led to years of full-length-mirror gazing and seeing nothing other than the fact that I did not have the body size of anyone you would find in a "back

....

1. Or paper towels. Or microwaves, for that matter. I'm just now realizing that these may be some of the reasons why I struggle to fit in with the majority of modern society.

to school" style guide. Eventually, I started to make a mental list of other flaws that I had, the list growing each time I looked in the mirror. With tears welling up in my eyes, I would stare at my reflection promise God that I would do anything he asked if he would just let me look more like the teens I saw in the magazines. I repeated this every day for years.

3) Attend a Mormon university and leave unmarried. (Preferably one with the unofficial motto: "A ring before spring or your money back.")

With eternal marriage always at the forefront of our minds, there was an unspoken rule that all the girls would spend their free time working out in the university's gym, aiming for a perfect body worthy of eternal commitment. The mandatory gym outfits (baggy gray men's T-shirts and dark-blue basketball shorts) were intended to keep you modest, but in reality they simply made made me look like a gargantuan cinder block dripping sweat while hogging the elliptical machine. I dutifully dedicated my time to the machinery and blue vinyl mats, determined to become a desirable wife for someone. Anyone.

When not at the gym, I would spend my evenings with Adam, an adorably nerdy, knobby-nosed piano player who would play *Bridge Over Troubled Water* in a way that made my chaste and desperate heart flutter. As we walked home after his two-person concert one night, I daringly collected all of the courage I had access to and confessed: "I really like you, y'know." This was met with silence, and then, eventually, an "Okay." It was the last word said for the rest of the trip to Kerr Hall's dormitory.

This was followed by a week of obsessive attempts to decipher his four-letter answer, often composing tabulated prose on my Xanga account for hours at a time. What exactly did "Okay" mean? Perhaps it was an agreement that the feelings were mutual? Maybe he meant that my confession was awesome and he was going to compose a seven-page love letter for me when he had the time to perfect it?

I later found out that it meant "That sucks, I'm in love with your roommate, Allison." The fact that we were similar in almost every way except that she was half my size was not lost on me.

4) Work for a misogynist with a penchant for obnoxious radio shows.

In my twenties, I worked as a kitchen manager in a downtown bakery. While the position by definition was something I loved, there were two unavoidable aspects that I was unaware of when I took the job. The first was to arrive at work before the sun came up to ensure that pastries were piping hot when the café opened, and the *other* was that I was required to occasionally spend those early morning hours with an egotistical general manager who loved four things:

1. Revving his motorcycle engine as loudly as possible when he parked out front

2. Wearing his long hair slicked back and tied with multiple scrunchies

3. Micromanaging the café employees he worked with by using primitive intimidation techniques

4. Blaring his favorite chauvinistic, 5:00 a.m. shock-jock radio show whenever working with the (often all-female) kitchen staff

Nothing about mixing muffin batter in the same room as this man was enjoyable, but collectively my friends and I found ways to shake off his hostility after our shifts had ended. There was one particular morning, however, when I simply couldn't find a way to rebound from those hours spent with him in the kitchen.

My hands were covered in flour, breaking up cold butter for the scone mixture while the radio show was playing through the speakers. Unable to physically tune out the vulgar conversation that was filling the kitchen, I continued to work as the radio jockey made a particularly smarmy comment about how he recently hurt his back while having sex with a "fat chick." My boss guffawed in response. Known for his attempts to make his name as the "Howard Stern of Tucson," this sort of conversation wasn't anything out of the ordinary for the host of this show, but in that moment I felt the shame of being a fat woman encompass me in a way it never had before. I couldn't breathe. I couldn't look up. I was "surrounded" by men who, though both plus size themselves, by laughing at this story reinforced that my body size was nothing but a punch line. One morning. One show. One comment. One manager. One moment I don't think I'll ever forget.

5) Wear cute clothing in public.
I was out on a weekend date with a dude I had been seeing for a while and was crushing pretty damn hard on. Dressed in a miniskirt, a skin-tight bedazzled Las Vegas tank top, and winged eyeliner that had never looked so sharp, there was no doubt in my mind that I was slaying that night and he was one lucky motherfucker.

After a few drinks at our favorite bar the two of us unlocked our bikes,[2] and a drunk sidewalk straggler accosted my date with a jeer: "So, you're out hunting for cellulite tonight?"

As a fat and vocal woman on the internet, I receive copious amounts of hate mail on a weekly basis, often with the subject line: "You're fat and ugly, just die already." The fat shaming itself wasn't

---

2. Applause, please, for riding a bicycle in a tight miniskirt and heels.

new, but that night, for some reason, it felt like a knife jabbed into my love-handled side.

Perhaps it was because earlier that day I had been feeling insecure about my body; real life is hard like that sometimes. Maybe it was because my date was rudely pulled into the ugly world of fat discrimination, where I felt he didn't belong. It was my world, one I still had shame around but dealt with alone. A world I didn't want to allow him any access to.

Or maybe it was because the comment came from a guy and was said to a guy, and this somehow made it hurt more; I was a sideshow freak not only unworthy of respect but also lacking enough value to have my presence acknowledged.

Most likely, though, it was a combination of all of these, in addition to my irrational fear that the person I was dating would suddenly realize that I was FAT now that it had been pointed out and would regret his life choices.[3] My shame and pain came from the fact that what had felt like my secret had been said out loud, and ignoring it was no longer an option.

Whether I liked it or not, my body confidence, unabashed miniskirt wearing, and ability to openly talk about my body size online did not protect me from the hurt that came from this comment.

I realized how vulnerable I still was.

6) Exist.

My mom and I share the same body type, one that, when we are both the same weight, makes our bodies look nearly identical. On a weekday evening, I came over after work to join my family for dinner and found myself standing in the kitchen when I overheard my dad

....

3. As if seeing me naked in bed earlier that week hadn't tipped him off about my size already.

comment on my mom's figure: "You look nice from behind, I guess. But not so much when you turn sideways." He doesn't remember saying this; it was just an offhand observation to him . . . but my mom and I remember. We remember the exact spot, the time of day, the lighting, the meal we were cooking, and I have always remembered the way I felt as I realized that this meant my body was unacceptable as well.

CHAPTER 3

I Was a Fat Kid

I SAT AT my mom's dining room table, a floral quilted scrapbook lying open in front of me, as I held a crinkly cellophane page between my fingers and stared at a photo of a young, grinning girl in a blue Girl Scout smock holding a paper in her hands with scrawling text that read: "Daisy Ending Certificate."

She was thin with messy blonde bangs and was surrounded by a few family members who were also beaming. This was obviously a celebratory affair, though it was likely as exciting as going to those graduation ceremonies they now hold for every elementary school grade, including kindergarten. In other words, my guess was that this Daisy graduation was boring AF.[1] Unless, of course, you were the one who had worked *their fingers to the bone* to earn those damn petal awards by practicing consideration and making crafts from

....

1. Let's be real here. Sitting in uncomfortable school seats to watch a painfully slow parade of dozens of kindergarteners (only one of whom you know) get lost while trying to cross a stage is something most people attend out of guilt and obligation, not for fun.

popsicle sticks *or* the parent who had managed to keep their kid alive throughout the process.

I smoothed the cellophane. The tag above the image, written in my mom's handwriting, read: "Jes, 5 years old. Glendale, CA." This twiggy, grinning, "I can make anything out of pipe cleaners" craftsman was me, and this fact left me completely shocked, totally alarmed and confused as hell.

This particular trip to visit my mom wasn't our usual Arbor Mist–chugging, catch-up-on-current-life-events kind. It had a specific purpose. I drove out to, yes, have a glass of headache-inducing sugar "wine," but after promising a chapter for this memoir about living in a fat body since childhood, my true motivation was to sit down, dust off a shelf full of scrapbooks, and glean all the inspiration I needed to write a clever chapter about growing up as a fat kid.

I had pulled out several photo albums and started with the one covered in pink flowers, excited for a nostalgic trip through my youngest years. I let the book fall open to a page, and my eyes roamed, looking for the fat kid that I had known for my entire life. She wasn't there. Instead, there was this small, blonde, Daisy-graduate version of me who was undoubtedly proud of learning how to count money and what courage meant. My memories of being a fat child didn't match this photo in the slightest. I didn't recognize her at all. Who the fuck was this kid?

I feel like I remember my childhood pretty vividly. I have recollections that are so clear and detailed that I once bet my brother twenty dollars when he disagreed with me about the color of the tablecloth my grandmother had in her kitchen when we were kids. It ended with a text response from my grandma that said yes, it in fact was light green with gold-trimmed edges and one oil stain and a "HA! FUCK YOU VERY MUCH NOW YOU OWE ME TWENTY BUCKS!" text to my brother from me. I may be an insufferable sore winner, but I am a winner with an exceptional memory nonetheless.

I remember a lot about little Jes, whose long blonde hair was always pulled back in a ponytail with a scrunchie and who wore lace-covered faux Keds while playing Chinese jump rope and made many memories of sheer happiness. Memories that come effortlessly to mind when I think about my childhood.

- I remember spending hot Tucson summer afternoons walking to the closest local library with a laminated card capable of checking out twenty-four books—then, the epitome of adulthood—clutched firmly in my hand. Hours were spent pulling out books from the children's section, flipping through the pages, and finally deciding on which two dozen to carry home in our laundry basket. Those books were deposited on my bed and read in less than two days. This process was repeated nearly every forty-eight hours for years.

- I remember the sound of my mother sitting down on the piano bench to perform several of Clementi's sonatas, all played half as fast as intended, some notes forever flat due to the warped wood; a result of the fact that our Wurlitzer seemed to always be placed under a swamp cooler. My mom learned these songs long before I was born, and they became my childhood's soundtrack that she played in the background until *Titanic* came out and I listened to "My Heart Will Go On" through my Walkman headphones on repeat while singing as loudly as possible. This continued until the CD "disappeared." The calming sonatas, however, are still played in my mother's house, eliciting tears of nostalgia and happiness in my eyes when listening even as an adult. The same piano playbook used since I was born still lives in my mom's current house, nearly forty years old, now missing the cover and with water-damaged pages and an age-worn spine.

- I remember watching every Rodgers and Hammerstein video over and over again until I had not only the song lyrics but also each actors lines memorized.[2]

- I remember the heavy scent that comes when coastal humidity mingles with the birch trees at my dad's family home in Los Angeles. This gummy air was punctuated with whiffs of cigarette smoke and the sulfuric smell of a just-opened can of cheap-ass Coors—both of which were always accompanied by the buzzing sports commentary that came from an old radio that was set next to a small television on mute; one offered the static detailed coverage of every move and the other showed the same in black and white. Poppy would use both pieces of technology in tandem, day in and day out, from the comfort of the brown and orange woven couch or his wooden porch chair. The night air in LA would be infused with whatever Nonny was cooking in the kitchen, often something that she learned to cook from her mother, who grew up on the family farm in Jalisco, Mexico. I'd spend nights on the living room floor, cross-legged, having my hair brushed by my aunt, baffled by her question about whether I had a "soft head or hard head." Blown away that an adult had no idea that all skulls are made out of hard bone, I answered the latter.[3]

....

2. While these movies usually brought me nothing but sheer joy, I held a fervent grudge against the actress who played Liesl von Trapp. I'll never forgive her for taking *my* part in *The Sound of Music*, even though it was filmed two decades before I was born. That *bitch*, amiright?

3. As it turns out, I have a very sensitive and *soft* head. My pride, which made me unwilling to acknowledge my ignorance, meant I spent years having my hair painfully pulled in silence while she assumed I couldn't feel a thing.

- I remember living in Mesa, where the harsh, hot air felt like you were inhaling dry ashes and our apartment had a swimming pool, which, to a seven-year-old, was the epitome of luxury. Chlorine, creaky shed hinges, and ducks will always remind me of the two-story apartment with a square-socketed hole built into the master bedroom's wall six feet above the floor. This concave shelf was likely designed to inspire awe but really just made it super fucking dangerous to place a heavy nineties television in. It was on that precariously placed TV that I watched Disney movies over and over, all of them promising that the good guys will always win.

- I remember playing Sim City using only the arrow keys, dressing up in my mom's two pairs of heels, and gossiping with my best friend Jessica while sitting on the cinder-block wall that divided our yards. We had the same name. We were the same age. We both had an affinity for salty dill vinegar, which always tasted the best when chugged out of a gallon jug.

I remember that no matter where we moved, pottery classes, sports, and family games of hide-and-seek after sunset were constant delights. Life smelled like flour freshly ground on the front porch and sounded like jazz with loon calls recorded over it. The living room dance parties got especially uninhibited when my mom turned on her vinyl record of Sheena Easton's *You Could Have Been With Me* (the third runner-up for my Childhood Soundtrack Mixtape). Church pews, youth activities, and hymns became an integral part our life, and we were all wonderful at it. I will admit that it's strange that my father, while definitely present during these moments, is oddly missing from my recollections, though this hasn't altered any of the magic I remember experiencing while young.

My mother worked tirelessly to make sure that my siblings and I felt happy and, most of all, safe. It's amazing to me when I consider how she did this, when the reality was that we spent the majority of my youth in devastating poverty. When the electricity was turned off, she would light candles and read us stories. She somehow succeeded in making bus rides to the grocery store and food bank feel like an adventure. When we acquired a small car, she took us to homeschool groups, to community plays, and on free or cheap adventures to bakeries, newspaper factories, and zoos. She enrolled us in every parks and rec class available.

We were overwhelmingly poor, sure, yet this never seemed to register for me as a negative thing. I enjoyed moving from house to apartment to another house in search of cheaper rent (and a more lenient landlord, let's be honest). Each move was another chance to decorate. I loved to walk to my grandmother's house (which smelled like dusty antiques and was always playing Frank Sinatra on an AM station in the background). I'd stay late on Saturday nights so we could lounge in recliners and watch Lawrence Welk together. I thought going to the "Bishop's Storehouse" (a food bank for poor but "devout" Mormons) was better than going to Costco. And when there was no money for Christmas presents, we made them; my Barbie bench, hand-crafted by my brother—essentially two splintery 2 x 4 pieces nailed together and painted blue—is still to this day one of the most cherished gifts I've ever received.

It's amazing to me how clearly I can remember all of these moments. The neighbors and their extended family. How the rain smelled different depending on the state we lived in. My favorite episode of *Reading Rainbow*. Which track came after "Telephone" on my mom's favorite cassette.

And along with all of these vibrantly idyllic memories, I vividly remember being a fat kid.

Fat kid as in preferring long sleeves during the summer, wrapping my thumb and middle finger around my wrist to prove to my classmates that I was simply "big boned," starting my first diet at thirteen, and knowing that I was broken from the moment I realized what it meant to be fat.

And this is why, as I sat at the table with my scrapbook in hand, I couldn't believe the picture of the little certificate owner in front of me. I decided this image must be an anomaly and that starting at the beginning of the album and moving forward in chronological order would confirm the fat-kid memories that I was so sure of.

I turned back to the first page.

A charming image of me as a baby greeted me on the first spread, and while I had an adorable Michelin Man–esque leg roll, I raised an eyebrow. The leg roll was cute, but I wasn't a particularly fat baby. I was positive the next picture would be more conclusive. The yellowed pages complained as I flipped: a small toddler now sans leg rolls, in black and white and wearing frilly white shorts I desperately wish I could find for my current wardrobe. The next page showed a rosy-cheeked four-year-old at a picnic, covered in dirt— she was also undeniably un-fat. I started to turn the pages a little faster. A small seven-year-old with enormous front teeth[4] wearing a giant green hair bow and a dress that looked like it was made out of a nineties couch. I started to hold my breath, my insides contracting with complete confusion. Little fat Jes. I thought I knew her well, but where *was* she?

Eight, a slight blonde posed at Olan Mills in a white baptismal dress in front of a pink-and-purple-streaked background. Nine, a

....

4. True story: I lost them both right before Christmas when I was eight, which gave me the obnoxious opportunity to sing "All I Want for Christmas Is My Two Front Teeth" for weeks. I still find this to be an impressive accomplishment.

small fourth grader line dancing at my country-themed birthday party (now with new, considerably smaller teeth). Ten, a Lindy Hop–themed birthday party. I was visibly pissed that Randy never showed up after promising to gift me a coveted Giga Pet, and it showed in a few of the photographs, but . . .

Still not fat. I was starting to become disoriented. I couldn't find the fat girl I had known my entire life *anywhere*. Who the *hell* was the girl in these pictures, and why did all of our memories match when our bodies clearly didn't?

A few more pages turned, and the book fell open to a picture of my twelve-year-old self posing for my softball league. We were the (mighty mighty!) Tucson Cyclones, and my preteen pride was evident as I awkwardly smiled at the camera, a slightly chubby girl holding a bat as if I were on home plate and ready to kick other twelve-year-old asses, complete with a giant zit, scratched until it matched the color of our maroon baseball caps.

There I was. That was the fat version of myself that I so clearly remembered. How was it possible that I didn't show up until midway through the album?

My mom was hanging her two new prisms in her living room window next to the dozen she had collected over the years, and I yelled for her to come look at my discovery.

She walked in, clapping her hands to rid them of dust, and leaned over the photo album I had prominently placed in the middle of the table.

"Holy shit, mom. *Did you know I wasn't a fat kid?*" I said, already scrambling to prove it, putting a finger in to hold the place of the sports picture.

Proof wasn't necessary, though. "Yeah, I know that, honey." I was short-circuiting, floored by the possibility that everyone else knew this but me. "Okay, but look at this softball picture—this is the first one where I *am* fat!" The photo was the confirmation I needed that I wasn't *completely* crazy, but I was still shell-shocked at the lack of evidence that I'd had a larger body before this sports portrait. I was more triumphant about being somewhat chubby in that moment than I can ever remember.

"Yes, Jes." She's always patient. "And that's when you hit puberty."

I immediately took pictures of these pictures. Proof, just in case I got home and started questioning this new reality again. A digital reminder of this slender childhood figure that challenged my body perception and my hyperawareness of my body. The hyperawareness I've felt ever since I can remember.

Perhaps the most alarming fact was that I had looked at that same album multiple times throughout my life. I had sat down with my mom as she proudly showed off her newly acquired scrapbooking skills; my whole family had been obsessed when subscriptions to rubber-stamp magazines were a hot thing. I had looked at *those* physical pictures for years and somehow still saw a fat kid. My mind was apparently so convinced that my body had always been contemptable by cultural standards that I, until this moment, had mentally superimposed another body size on top of my own.

I had been so impacted by a belief I'd been taught from a young age that my mind had ignored and warped hard visual proof. Until now, even dozens of printed photos didn't seem to portray the body I actually inhabited, only the one I somehow believed I had.

I grappled with the now obvious truth: I wasn't a fat child physically. I was only a fat child in my mind.

My defective perception of my fatness was omnipresent in every experience I'd had as a child, even those magical picture-book moments I so clearly remember. Skipping home from the library, excited about my armful of books ... while fat. Visiting a newspaper factory and staring in awe at the machines ... while fat. Looking up in wonder at the Disneyland castle that seemed to be enormous...while fat. Every magical memory, vivid and loved...all while fat.

My entire life subconsciously revolved around my body, which meant that my world was seen through the lens of being a fat kid. When "Fat Kid" *is* your identity, and then you discover twenty years later that you were never who you'd thought you were, you're left at age thirty-one with little else besides a mentally insurmountable mindfuck that feels impossible to untangle.

Body dysmorphia. I suppose this was it, exemplified. That seems to be the only term I can think of to describe when a person has no fucking idea what they actually look like no matter how many times they look in the mirror, have their picture taken, or have their body described.

I have been "my body" my entire life. I've experienced decades through the lens of being an undeniable fat girl ever since I understood what fat was. And yet, for the majority of my life, I didn't *actually* know what my body looked like. My physical identity was a fabricated lie that eventually, as I became older, led to an unshakable self-hatred that ultimately became a fundamental part of my life and personality.

The joke was on me. I wasn't a fat kid, and it took me damn near twenty years to figure it out.

"Mom but, I mean...did *you* tell me I was a fat kid?" I stumbled over the words, grasping for any sort of logical reason for how I had deceived myself for so long. As a fairly intelligent person who has been aggressively educating myself about and challenging weight myths for half a decade, I was unsure how this had happened. How had I found myself at the dining room table, being schooled about myself by Kodak prints?

"I didn't," was my mom's reply. "I really don't think I thought about it that much, to be honest. Bodies just weren't on my radar..." she trailed off.

I believed her. My mom's complicated history with abuse, weight, and the strong presence of Christianity's aversion to anything other than complete chastity made this possible. Her body had become an unsafe place in which to exist over the years, and so she actively sought safety everywhere else. She married a Mormon man, clutching to the promise of eternal salvation, used clothing to hide every inch of her body as directed by the church, and gained weight through cycles of depression and a willingness to fade into the background. In her world a fat body was an invisible body. An invisible body was a safer body. And the safest body of all was the fat one you completely disassociate with and leave in the corner while you search for your life's meaning everywhere else.

Her children's bodies, then, became simply the thing that held us together. Her concerns went no further than *You're covered in dirt and should probably shower. When was the last time you changed your socks? Time to braid your hair for school, we're running late. Did you have lunch today?* and other parental worries focused purely on our day-to-day survival.

This seemed to be a wonderfully neutral approach, though her disconnect from our appearance likely played a part in letting me wear orange socks to elementary school. As a ten-year-old who didn't need to be "cool, cool" but still didn't want to be really uncool, this was a highly regrettable decision.

I left my mom's house confused, slightly dazed, and thoroughly baffled by the day's unexpected discovery. My childhood had been lived through the lens of a fat body that hadn't actually existed. How could my clear memories be so untrustworthy? I shrugged off my confusion, figuring that this inability to view myself in an honest way must have come from my obsession with becoming Ariel and the other Disney princesses I aspired to be. Maybe I felt like my body had always been fat because I loved to sketch figures from a "Drawing Comics" how-to book from the fifties where every figure's thinness was greatly exaggerated.

It all seemed too simplistic, but I didn't have any other explanation. I shook my head as I walked back out to my car, my phone full of proof that I had been wrong about one of the most fundamental influences in my life. I pulled on my seat belt, turned the Disney Pandora station back on,[5] and drove away.

5. Old habits die *hard*.

CHAPTER 4

I Wasn't Actually a Fat Kid

I GREW UP KNOWING MY dad as two people, and two people only:

1. The obsessive dieter who would spend his days describing the long list of foods he couldn't eat to anyone who listened and then each night would jog in circles on our green living room rug, making sure to follow the white braided outline, lap after lap, sure that this diet would be the one that worked.

2. The man who closed all the blinds and sat on the couch, consuming containers of ice cream while demanding that his children bring him another can of Pepsi until our trash bin was full.

He would start a new drastic diet, lose a significant amount of weight, ride the high of obedience and social praise, and then promptly gain it all back. This was followed by resuming his canned-and frozen-food diet. I cannot remember a time during my young life when this two-sided lifestyle wasn't the norm.

Only occasionally did these personalities overlap, when he would draw the curtains and devour soda and Neapolitan ice cream while watching *The Biggest Loser*, which in hindsight explains everything about my father's body-image issues. He felt desperately out of control of his body, his emotions, his life, and never believed that he had the ability to become a "better" person on his own.

Better is a loaded word, though. I know enough to realize that in America, for the longest time, a "manly man" could hold his head up high and know his worth if he had money and power. Born into a life of chronic poverty, my dad was never given the chance to have either of those things, unable to hold a job for more than a few months due to unreliability and never offered self-esteem by his parents or others. And thus he turned to the thing that he felt was the only thing within his control: his body.

....

I also grew up knowing that my dad despised me.

This wasn't a secret even within our home. I had to come to terms with the fact that he, a hyperconservative and passive misogynist raised in a house with a domineering father and docile mother, feared loud and opinionated females. I have been one of those females since I could speak. After watching his treatment of my mother and sister (both detested for their similar outspokenness and un-wrangleable spirits), I simply accepted that this was the way things were at home, though my acceptance didn't come without resentment or emotional anguish.

If I push myself into agony-inducing recollection, I *can* remember the years of emotional abuse, but for years I have made the purposeful choice not to.

I attribute my success in avoiding the past emotional pain to my creative ability to remove all personal connection to the memories that include him and rewrite them into what feels like a fictional story about a character. Blocking his presence from my life was surprisingly effective, though it offered nothing in the way of healing. It also explains my father's strange invisibility in my happy childhood memories; perhaps I made sure he wasn't invited into that story and instead was written into another series—one that couldn't touch my more idyllic narrative.

The book in which he appeared was written about a different blonde-haired, violin-playing girl. A book that I am able to close, put up on a high shelf, and walk away from.

After leaving for college, I found that there *was* a possibility of my finding civil ground with my dad, but it could only happen if we were 1,016 miles away from each other and only communicated by phone. After completing several years at BYU–Idaho, I returned home and purposefully distanced myself from my entire family by rebelling against every single religious restriction I had learned while growing up; there were many. I smoked cheap-ass cigarettes, drank hard alcohol, had sex with countless questionable individuals, tried mushrooms by cooking them in an omelet, snorted a shit-ton of coke mixed with aspirin,[1] and got multiple tattoos. Much of my rebellion was the natural 180-degree swing that humans experience after living a hyper-restrictive lifestyle. Some (though not my poor mother) would argue that these exploratory actions were needed, even healthy. Regardless of why I made these decisions, it built an invisible blockade that for a while broke my mom's heart (which was still clinging to eternal salvation as a way out of a hellish life) and also conveniently distanced me from my dad's damaging thumb. He couldn't control me as his child if I was no longer a child who was out of control.

....
1. Note to coke dealers: Ex-Mormons fresh off the God Boat will always be gullible. Be nice.

It's shocking to realize that to this day, I've only had two real and honest conversations with my dad in my entire life.

One happened on a muggy summer night seven years ago, when I closed my bedroom door, sat cross-legged on my rumpled bed, and angrily dialed his number, both shouting and sobbing on the phone, for the first time in my life voicing my anger at his deliberate complicity and undeniable responsibility in a diagnosis that had become apparent over the years of one-on-one therapy, intensive outpatient dialectical behavioral therapy, and countless appointments with other behavioral health professionals. It was terrifying to verbally share over the phone to my father that he had played one of the most significant roles in my now unignorable emotional scarring and caused the development of a mental illness that was learned through experiencing extended emotional abuse. A mental illness that was now so prevalent that it hindered my ability to fully flourish.

He also cried, a bewildering reaction that I was unfamiliar with, his voice cracking as he acknowledged and apologized for his abusive parenting. He promised to do better. He could do better; *he would do better.* And I believe that he truly believed it. But, still emotionally unable to fulfill the promises he longed to keep, they became hollow assurances that were never met with follow-through.

For nearly a decade, I continued to consciously push my father out of my mind as well as my physical space. This was made simpler by my parents' divorce, and he, while still at our regular family gatherings, remained easy to keep at a distance. I declined invitations to plan his parties, would send obligatory short texts on his birthday and Father's Day, and made small talk when necessary. I used rage—the easiest emotion for me to feel—to keep him as far away as possible.

He continued his life of compulsive dieting followed by extreme weight loss and then the ever-dependable weight gain . . . this time, from the other side of town. He continued to struggle to keep a job, oftentimes borrowing money from my siblings. He would show up unannounced at my mom's house, making himself comfortable on the couch before listing his requests. And even though I attempted to distance myself from these events and instead focused my world around my interests, jobs, dating life, and other narcissistic things, I would occasionally hear about his latest visit, with details about how much he was struggling.

Highly sensitive and empathic, I am often unable to filter out other people's emotional pain. And even though he continued to shamelessly take from others while making his empty promises, left the mortgage on a single mother with five children, and was handed multiple opportunities but rejected them because they were too difficult, hearing about his suffering left me on a constant internal battlefield. I cried often, fighting between heartbroken empathy for a person in pain and my armored decision that I owed him nothing because of the pain he had caused me personally.

I cried out of sadness because life was unkind to both of us.

I cried out of anger because life was unkind to both of us.

I've also been known to cry at the ending of *Finding Dory*, every time I think about homelessness, when Jayna Brown got the Gold Buzzer on *America's Got Talent* for singing "Rise Up," after cursing at my dog when he knocked coffee on my laptop, because I hurt his feelings, and even while I read love letters from my partner.

It's an understatement to say that I cry a lot.

But through the tears I still slogged on, firm in my conviction that his toxicity would no longer take up space in my life. Polite in person, disconnected otherwise, and never letting my guard down when I was around him; the one-dimensional rage served its purpose. We had vocally fought my whole life. This disconnect wasn't new; it was now just silent.

I've come to realize in the last few years that forgiveness isn't something that we owe anyone. Instead, it's something you do for yourself so that those toxic feelings have permission to leave. Forgiving my father was something I never felt was necessary for his sake, but perhaps someday—should I be able to manage it—it could be healing for me.

I know we're all given a proverbial hand of cards when we're born. We don't have control over what life we're born into, which body we have, what brain chemistry we inherit, or what our family looks like. Because of this, I do my best to release people from the expectation of perfection.

I have to draw a line for my sanity, though, and that line is when people's actions cause harm to others—especially chronic, repeated harm that isn't or won't be addressed.

It's here that I leave. It's here that I encourage other people to leave the relationships that are harmful. It's here that I encourage those hurting people around them to find a professional who can assist without being a direct and personal target. It's here that the person being wounded gets to step away and other people with less personal investment step in. In this way, I feel that the line I drew between my father and me, while painfully blunt, was needed.

I've carried scars for decades. Many of these scars were given to me (consciously and subconsciously) by my dad. Yes, I've spent nearly a decade unraveling them, naming them. But they still show, the deepest ones given to me as a child, powerless, dependent, without any way to defend myself.

It's painful to do, but I also have to acknowledge that my dad was once a child as well. Also powerless, dependent, and without the skills to keep him safe from an emotionally distant father who never recovered from war. From poverty and a mother who didn't know how to advocate for his safety.

For decades, my harsh line in the sand was safety; I felt justified in removing my dad from my life. I didn't feel like I deserved any more harm than I had already received. I was going to fight for my right of emotional safety for as long as I needed to.

And then somehow, surreptitiously, as life is known to do, everything changed.

I started to notice him aging—shrinking, becoming frailer and consequently more vulnerable. He would come to family dinners as always, but he moved slower, no longer talking over people or forcing his way into anyone's private life. Soon he was wearing a heart pump, explaining his new medical condition, how stints worked, and why he needed one.

There was something about hugging him and feeling the machinery strapped to his back so that he could monitor his condition, and knowing that he couldn't survive on his own without a tube in his abdomen, that broke down every wall I had built over my lifetime.

This man in front of me was no longer a threat to my healing. Instead, he was fading every time I saw him, becoming a sadder, softer shadow of his former self. And every time I saw the fading, my anger and line started to fade a bit too.

My boundaries became unnecessary; my walls, coarse. This was no longer a person who wanted to or even *could* hurt me. This was a man too fragile to start a fight. The only confrontation that could be brought to the table now was by me.

And I could not fight an unarmed man.

It caused me irrepressible sadness that I couldn't force myself to *not* feel, though I tried. This was the man who had hurt me my entire life, whose rage and hatred had been thrown at me over and over again. And while he only slapped my face with his hand once in my life, every day the meaning behind that physical slap was reinforced through each interaction we had.

And now, he is in the hospital more often than not. Going in for a heart checkup and staying for gallbladder surgery. Having gallbladder surgery then staying for an intestinal infection. Lying day after day in a hospital bed, not alone in a physical sense, because family members visit here and there. But there is truth in the idea that you can have a million people surrounding you and, because of the life you've chosen, still be very much alone.

I started texting every day. It was new, scary, and all I could bring myself to do. I made sure he had what he needed, read his long explanations about how horrible the hospital food was and what other procedures were happening. I asked if he was being visited enough, and he assured me he was. But there is something about watching a person slowly disappear—their energy, then their color, then their body—that pushes you, unwillingly, to the edge of an emotional canyon and forces you to look, to see the vastness held within it and realize that you've explored so little. That life isn't infinite but *is* monumental, and if you don't start exploring now, you are going to miss some of the most important sights. The feeling of being consumed with grief at the idea of losing someone you've known for so long yet hardly understand . . . that feeling changes you. Being faced with visual reminders of human mortality has always affected me, jolting my consciousness and propelling me toward action—action I could have been taking all along.

The thought of him alone, sick, and dependent in a hospital left me in tears every night. My partner Andy occasionally asked if I wanted to call him, looking for any solution that would ease my pain and stop the flood that wouldn't stop pouring from my eyes. Each time I would shake my head. The act of calling him, as innocuous as it was, was beyond my emotional capacity.

But one night, after weeks of behind-the-scenes anguish, I dug up strength from god knows where and dialed his number, finally ready to have a second conversation.

I listened while he explained all of his treatments in lengthy detail. About how he couldn't eat spicy sausages anymore and how he was happy to be sleeping after not being able to for a week. I silently listened, tears rolling down my cheeks, until he had finished.

A moment of silence went by before I said, in a small and quivering voice, "Dad, I'm so sad you're in the hospital and not doing well. . . . I'm just . . . so sad." It wasn't much, but it was the bravest I could be in that moment.

"Thanks, Jes. I'm really okay though." His voice sounded ten years older than he was, so much like his father's.

"I just hate seeing you feeling weak and suffering and I . . . I just need you to know that I know that I was so angry at you for so long, and I'm not angry or upset with you anymore."

I was sobbing at this point, my words insufficient. I continued anyway. "I mean, I know you hated me growing up, but I just can't handle seeing you like this, and I wanted to make sure you knew that I loved you."

He was also sobbing at this point.

"I never hated you," he croaked. "Never. I just had a really hard time because I saw a lot of myself in you, and I blamed myself for it." Words were obviously failing him as well, but the decades of previously unspoken sadness finally being voiced kept us on the phone.

"What do you mean? I thought you resented me because I was an opinionated woman and you had a hard time with those. What could you possibly see in me that reminded you of yourself?" We couldn't have been more different.

"Well, y'know," he said, "I was lazy, and when I saw you being lazy too it upset me, and so I took it out on you. It wasn't you, though, you have to know that. The problem was me. I know that now. . . . I just didn't know what to do about it back then."

My ears didn't register anything after that confession. All sound was replaced by that phenomenon of quiet ringing that only happens when your brain hits maximum capacity with so much power that your senses become numb. Somehow, the world stopped making noise and then the ringing turned into deafening silence, though I was semi-aware that my dog was barking in an attempt to incite the cats, that Andy's Netflix show was filling the house with British accents, and that our five box fans were anything but quiet. I sat in shock, hearing nothing and completely unsure of what I was feeling.

This was the first time in my life that I had heard anything about this. It blindsided me. I felt not only disoriented but also significantly hurt by the insinuation that I had been seen as lazy for my entire life.

"Dad, I wasn't a lazy kid," I said desperately. "I was one of those annoying straight-A kids who got a job and went to college at sixteen and played every instrument and sport imaginable. You have to remember that, right? And I mean, even if I *was* lazy, I was just a child . . . y'know?"

Those memories and achievements seemed unforgettable to me. As a kid who clung to being the best overachiever I could be as penance for my failure of a body, if anything, I grew up staying *too* busy.

Nothing was making sense.

"I know, I know," emotion choked his words as he tried to voice them. "I just told you that I saw that you were lazy and I thought you had learned it from me and I . . . I felt really upset that it was my . . . fault." He paused, likely hearing those words said out loud for the first time, just as I was.

And I suddenly understood.

His words had to be deciphered, I realized; they were still heavily coded. He was speaking a language that in my life was now primitive and clumsy. But while I was rusty from lack of practice, I used to be fluent in it. After hearing the intonation in my dad's explanation, the truth struck me with so much force I could barely breathe.

Fat.

He saw me as fat, both when I wasn't fat as a child and also when I gained weight during puberty and beyond. He thought that I had learned it from him, and he was upset that it was his fault.

"Dad, you obviously hated your body and struggled to change it for years. Were you worried that you'd be another failure if you had a fat kid?"

He was thinking, I could tell, struggling to put together a better way to say something. He couldn't come up with the right words this time, though.

"Yes."

This had nothing to do with laziness. *Lazy* was just a synonym for *fat* in the all-too-familiar bigoted world I continue to live in. *Fat* and *lazy* are too often connected though unrelated.

He married my mom and adopted me when I was only two, so we weren't biologically related. We shared only history, not genes.[2] But even this reality didn't stop the hatred he directed toward my body, the intensity with which he hated himself overriding all logic. He couldn't seem to change his body, and he also failed to change mine. This was why I had hated my body my entire life, the reason I truly believed I was fat and broken. This is why I expected to see a fat child in all of those images I searched through. This is why I forced myself to live a smaller life for decades in order to compensate for the largeness of my body. Because of his internalized fatphobia and self-hatred, I had been taught from the age of two that my body was unacceptable, and consequently I was insignificant. Neither were or are true, and at thirty-one I'm grateful to

....

2. Which leaves me with a lot of questions about my biological father and his genetic makeup, someone I have no memory of. Pete, should you read this, I would love a response to that letter I wrote you ten years ago. That would be supercool.

at least know the reason behind the body dysmorphia I have felt for nearly three decades.[3]

It's pretty unusual to learn how to internalize diet culture and physical self-hatred from your father, yet he was the catalyst for my lifetime of internalized fatphobia. I believed for most of my life that I was and had always been a spherical monstrosity, and this stemmed from *his* fear of personal failure. And while it was his self-hatred that had filled our home as I grew up, it clearly became my problem as well—the reason I found myself flipping through scrapbooks months before, looking for a fat kid that never existed.

The strange thing is that I, a writer who covers body-image topics almost daily, still have a limited understanding of what being fat actually means. I often find myself asking, so *when* did I become fat? Like, *actually* fat?

There are all kinds of terms within the body acceptance movement to differentiate sizes of fat: Small Fat, Big Fat, Super Fat, and sometimes just Fat. And as my body continues to gain weight over the years, I find myself questioning whether I was actually fat when I was in my early twenties. Or was I finally fat as a hipster a few years later? Did the weight gain during my first long-term relationship make me legitimately fat? My second relationship ended because my body changed, and also around that time I started blogging about body image. Was being designated as fat by my partner or the internet the moment I became officially fat? What about afterward, when I was single and dating? I was convinced I was fat then, but looking back at pictures, that particular body seems so slender compared to my current shape. The concept of *fat shaming* is now liberally claimed by models whose bodies are a third of my size, and the definition of who is and isn't actually fat has become blurry. Now that the BMI's

....

3. To (embarrassingly) quote Marvel's character Vision, "I want to understand. The more I do, the less it controls me." Amen, red android dude. Amen.

relevance has been disproven repeatedly, there doesn't seem to be a standard for what constitutes a fat body, and this leaves me questioning how long "actual" fatness has been a part of my life. When did I cross the "unacceptable body" line? And does it really matter?

I am pretty sure of two things at this point, and one is that I am, at this current moment, fat. I still don't know what category of "fat" I belong in but I *am* fat. I'm the kind of fat that people will no longer deny when I state it. I'm stranger-jaw-dropping fat. Look-of-concern-on-clinical-faces fat. Embarrassed-for-you-so-I'll-smile-while-you-walk-by fat. Whisper-as-you-leave-a-restaurant fat. Side-eye-hoping-I'm-not-sitting-next-to-you-as-I-board-the-plane fat.

The kind of fat that gets a comment on Twitter moments after midnight on New Year's Eve that says, "CONGRATULATIONS ON FINALLY BECOMING DEATH FAT."[4]

The second thing I am semisure of is that I will never be thin again. I haven't worn straight-size clothing since I was a preteen, and even though I've tried every magic trick I could think of to shrink my body, I am still my now-acknowledged "Fat." I highly doubt that thinness will ever be a part of my life again.

....

I suppose there has been a third honest conversation between my dad and I—the most recent one where I sat on his couch cross-legged and anxious and read a printed-out version of this chapter to him. I wasn't sure why I was there or what the point was of reading these words to him in person; I just knew I needed to do it.

He listened silently while I wiped away tears. Voicing these specific and painful memories felt impossible, but I pushed through

....

4. I was impressed with myself at how much I seemed to have accomplished between 12:00 a.m. and 12:01 a.m. Definitely a productive start to a promising year. Those celebratory fireworks were obviously for me.

them all. I finished reading and looked at him, lips trembling, unsure what to do next. I found myself overwhelmed by a confusing mixture of emotions—intense compassion for the man in front of me but also confidence that my harsh dissection of our history was completely truthful.

Unable to read his face, I broke the silence. "What do you think, Dad?"

He spent a few minutes thinking. "Well, I think you have to process your past in whatever way you need to, Jes. It's probably good for you to go through it and write what you're feeling."

Taken aback by the softness in his answer, I sat in silence for a moment. "Is there anything you want changed? Is there anything that hurt you? I don't want to hurt you . . ." I was crying again, unsure why this relationship was still so hard to talk about, to write about.

"I am a little hurt, because I was there for you too when you were younger Jes," was his honest answer. "I guess you don't remember, but we used to flood the house with water fights, bowl until we were sore, and take my old truck through monsoon puddles while you and your brothers sat in the bed of my truck so you could get drenched. I would pick you up when your shifts ran late and the buses stopped running. I was the one who came to your house when you lived in that downtown house and were suicidal. I was the one who showed up and removed the pills and alcohol and took you home to recover. I also salvaged your hair when you were eight and confused a handful of Vaseline for styling gel." He chuckled. "We had good moments together too, you know."

He was right.

What was the real reason that he was absent in my childhood memories? How much of my inability to reconcile with my body is attributable to my father, and what percentage comes from other equally complex influences? How the hell did this unspoken fatphobia manage to dig its claws in so deep that it is taking a lifetime to undo the damage? Why did I remember sitting on my bed surrounded by piles of pills and vodka bottles but not who walked through the door? Why had it taken us this long to acknowledge this part of our shared history? Why is it so crucial to rip open old wounds so they can properly heal? Why is mending twenty-year-old harm *such a BITCH*? And how the hell did I manage to confuse a tub of Vaseline for a tube of L.A. Looks gel?

There are still so many questions I'm unable to answer, but even still I've had a few realizations that allow me to move forward, albeit slowly.

My body holds my mystery but no longer defines my entire identity. My jean size doesn't have anything to do with my value as a human. My body is not an indicator of my worth. My body is not meant to be a mirror for other people's insecurities. My body is something that I am working toward accepting, and once I'm able to find some neutral space inside of me I will be able to continue allowing it to disappear into the background as much as society lets me, and then some. No longer something to be fixed, all I want to do is simply engage, experience, and love my life. My body is a vehicle that can take me toward that happiness.

And maybe, just maybe, it can also be the conversational bridge that allows me to finally mend the relationship I have with my father.

CHAPTER 5

....

The Fat Cowgirl Position

I'M CONVINCED THAT serious, long-term relationships are the hardest. And it's not because of the cohabitation or cleanliness mismatches, or because of the co–budget finagling that must inevitably happen or having to learn how to love your partner's trash-eating, sock-destroying dog. It's not even because of figuring out the "how do we make this work" communication skills that often differ. No. It's because inevitably, someday, you're probably going to have sex with the lights on.

Having sex, for many people (even straight-sized), isn't just "having sex." It's a complicated cha-cha you do with multiple parts of your body during which you mentally juggle a narrative that always seems impossible to drown out. *Is this okay? Do I look okay? Am I doing this right? Are they enjoying this? Am I enjoying this?* I know this because sex is one of my favorite topics of discussion, and my non–plus sized friends, like myself, don't have any boundaries. Having sex for *fat* women, though. . . . I can't help but feel like it's a little different. It's not just a complicated cha-cha; it's a fucking dance marathon during which you hope to god your partner doesn't notice when you breathe heavy and armpit sweat starts to appear. These may be normal things that happen during any physical activity, but when you're fat they become physical indicators that you *hope to god* aren't silently attributed to your fatness by your partner. Your mental narrative (in *addition* to the ones above, I might add) goes something like this: *Lord, I hope my stomach isn't in the way. Is it ruining this angle? Are my arms jiggling? Can I do that position, or is my ass too big? How does that even work? Can they see my rolls? Do they care about my rolls? Of course they don't care about my rolls, they're having sex with me.* Or maybe *they wish they weren't having sex with me, and I should jump ship before they change their mind mid-bone. Should I be asking them if they're thinking of changing their mind in the middle of sex? Is that weird? Is having sex with me weird? Is this running conversation in my head about everything except my enjoyment weird?* Or my personal favorite worry, which forever plays on repeat while riding on top of my partner: *Jesus Christ, am I breaking their rib cage and crushing their organs? Should I be calling an ambulance? I kind of need to know this right now; the paramedics take forever to arrive and I really don't want to kill anyone today.* It's a real thing.

I'd like to think that most fat women don't have this experience while having sex, but because 1) I can't find enough articles on the subject to prove otherwise; and 2) all my fat friends have shared similar neuroses, I have to conclude that more of us are thinking this way while naked than I care to count. And this is why we've all learned to turn the lights off—sometimes we just want to have sex without worrying about the way we look. This makes daylight, in turn, the ultimate enemy.

I met Klark on Craigslist (a normal part of my life at that point), and the reasons why I fell head over heels for him seem hazy these days. He had stalker tendencies—the kind where he finds you on Facebook and goes to music shows he thinks you might be at based on the pages you like, hoping to "accidentally" bump into you there.

(I chose to find it romantic.) He often wondered aloud if the only reason I wanted to date him was because no one else would. (I used this as a treasured opportunity to assure him that this was *not* the case, as I was a catch.) He also held me personally responsible for the success of our relationship because he was still in the midst of a hellish divorce that I had "caused." (His willingness to endure a gruesome divorce meant I was *extra special*, I convinced myself.) But regardless of why we started dating, we did. We texted every waking moment until we started to see each other every day. We saw each other every day until we started seeing each other every night. And we shared every night together until he said, "Y'know, I'm going to be moving out of my house and will need a roommate so . . ." and then promptly moved into my minuscule one-bedroom apartment with its brightly painted yellow living room and hallway kitchen. As in, the kitchen was literally in the hallway. (A note to my future self: If your house doesn't have adequate space for a mini-oven and micro-wave, it probably doesn't have room for two people, a cat, and an excessive amount of art supplies.) Looking back (20/20, y'all), I see how this was the second-worst decision of my life[1] and a questionable beginning to a questionable relationship. Nevertheless, my yellow shoebox apartment became ours, and we tried our optimistic hand at cohabitation . . . all within a month of meeting. I wasn't joking when I confessed a minute ago that I've made some bad decisions.

Now, I believe that almost every person has a loveable side to them, that we all have parts of ourselves that are beautiful. We also all have dark and dangerous sides. Unfortunately for some, though, when we're looking for companionship above all else, we decide

---

1. The first being the decision to sit on my grandmother's exercise bike when I was seven. My conscienceless younger brother pushed me onto the metal frame, and I ended up in a tub for days with a bruised tailbone. Bruised tail-bones are excruciating, and I've held a grudge against stationary bikes (and my brother) ever since.

that the rather sparse percentage of "good" is more than enough! I mean, maybe this person is 70 percent messed up, but they're actually 30 percent awesome, and that's pretty close to 50 percent, which becomes 100 percent if you round up. *Holy shit, this person is perfect! Let's get married!* And the red flags whiz on by. I am obviously speaking from a great deal of experience, as I too am a red flag ignorer who also happens to be a professional rounder-upper.

Once I had been dating Klark for a few months, and despite the fact that he seemed to be into me and my body (meaning, we had sex sometimes, and I got the occasional semi-reassuring "I wouldn't be with anyone I didn't find attractive, okay?"), I couldn't help but have the lingering (read: soul-crushing) fear that I wasn't enough in bed, that I needed to work harder to keep him. After all, in my easily duped mind, thin women (and all thin bodies) were a blessing to men in bed; they were an honor to have sex with and needed to do little more than show up to keep their partner satisfied. Thanks to my deeply internalized and unshakeable fatphobia, I wholeheartedly believed that if a thin person showed up in the bedroom, their partner needed nothing else. And because of the same fatphobia (with a supplemental side of learned misogyny), I felt that as a fat person, this was not the case for me. This led to a desperate need to compensate for my weight, to remind Klark that I was definitely worth some rumpled sheets and maybe a drop or two of sweat. This need was eventually exacerbated (and reaffirmed) by his saying, "I don't know . . . sex is really exhausting when I do all the work." At thirty-one, I've just learned the term "Pillow Princess," a reference to women who do little in bed and expect much. I didn't have the vocabulary then to explain my fears about becoming "that" kind of sex partner, but I was determined to never become *that*. I couldn't *afford* to become *that*. I wouldn't be worth staying with if I became a needy lover.

This fear led me to read a million books about giving "the blow-job he'll never forget!" (actually, six, but one was called *Tickle His Pickle,* and I knew that if that didn't help me I should stop looking). Eventually, it led me to Google, where I typed in anything I could think of that could make me into a partner worth undressing. I spent hours searching fanatically for "How to ride cowgirl," "Cowgirl position how to," and even "So I'm a cowgirl, now what?"

The most solid advice I could find was *Cosmopolitan* telling me to pretend I was on a pogo stick.[2] This not only seemed unnerving to me as sex advice but also brought up distressing memories involving the childhood toy that was popular in the 1990s. Every time I tried a pogo stick as a child I ended up with raw elbows and laughter from those around me. All in all, NOT. HELPFUL. COSMO.

But even though *Cosmo* is initially responsible for ruining my sex life before it ever started (I'll never forget the traumatizing article I read in college titled "How to Look Thinner in Bed," which was basically *just lie flat and suck it in.* This "suck it in while having sex" advice was seared into my memory for years. I only recently realized how ludicrous this suggestion was), it was the only advice I could find, so I attempted it with the dysfunctional devotion that most people give their diet on January 1st. *He will finally be satisfied at last!* I was already internally celebrating. *It was a basic trick, right? Women were just born knowing how to do this, right? Pogo stick . . . right?* Hell. Fucking. No.

My eager attempt to implement this substandard advice was cut short after trying it, not loving it, and picking up on the pretty obvious fact that he didn't love it either. There's a good chance he

....

2. I mentioned this advice much later to my friend Adiba, who met the suggestion with genuine horror. "Ride like a pogo stick. OMG no. Never. Not even for a thin girl. No. You will puncture your fucking uterus. Please add that in your book; it's important. You slide and glide on that shit. Not ride and die." And now we all know.

may have yawned; I'm unsure. "I feel like this isn't working," I quietly said, mustering up every ounce of vulnerability I could while looking down, my entire body feeling excruciatingly exposed. His response was defensive, like a knife to my (oh God, so shameful) gut: "Well, then it's because my stomach is too big, or yours is." There was an uncomfortably long pause. And then a double pause for a maximum reminder that *obviously* this was my fault. It couldn't be his fault. His body was considerably slimmer than mine, which indubitably meant that *my* body was the broken one. *Of course* I was the broken one; my body has been wrong since my earliest memory. This was just another example of physical failure, something I was all too familiar with. The shame encompassed me until I felt like I was on the verge of having a panic attack, so I, in a state of complete mortification, climbed off of his body and never again attempted that position with him. In fact, I didn't attempt it for years, even after our partnership ended.

I proceeded to (miraculously) survive that painful relationship, even after we stopped having sex. Our miserable celibacy period lasted well over a year and a half, despite the fact that we were living together and fell asleep next to each other each night, me trying to hide my tears and muffled sobs every time. I was convinced that I was the problem in the relationship; that if I were to do something different, things would get better. I was unaware at the time that this was simply a manifestation of my crucial need for control. That by convincing myself that it was *me*, I was convincing myself that I still had the power to fix it. If it was me that needed to change, I could do that! Absolutely! No problem! I could absolutely fix this.

It's possible that the only thing harder to look at than "you are the defective part of this relationship" is looking at the reality that maybe the two of you simply aren't good for each other. That maybe you are both broken in incompatible ways. That maybe his childhood trauma made him incapable of authentic intimate connection, and maybe your childhood trauma made you need authentic intimate connection a little too much. That maybe your overwhelming need for love was triggering his excruciating insecurities, which would cause him to pull away, which made you then crave love more and more, until the overwhelming turned into suffocating. Rinse, repeat, cry yourself to sleep. Sometimes the reality is that even though you invested years trying to make it work, maybe you had no business being in this relationship at all.

The relationship continued to disintegrate until I had very few tears left.

One morning we lay in bed (in that goddamn daylight), and after an agonizing amount of uncomfortable silence he rolled over to face me. His eyes, though looking straight at me, were remarkably distant as he explained how he had been observing his close friend who was in a visibly miserable marriage. He asserted that he had already endured one long and joyless partnership within his last marriage and the last thing he wanted was another one. I felt paralysis consuming not only my body but my heart as I realized my biggest fears were being confirmed. He was leaving, and because of this my life was obviously over. Over as in auction off your belongings and buy a plot next to your grandfather's, Jes. There is clearly nothing to live for anymore.

The tears that I had thought were gone somehow replenished themselves and started to pour. How could this be happening? How could *I* be the one being left? *I'm the one who does the dumping, asshole. I'm the one that leaves relationships, not the other way around.* I had always prided myself on this, as though it were an indicator of my worth and superior value as a partner. No one leaves me, thank you very much. I open and close the front door myself. But by that logic, Klark's leaving me meant my relationship currency was now nonexistent. It implied that I now had absolutely zero worth as a human and that this breakup conversation was the beginning of the end of my soon to be sad and lonely life. I was sure of it.

We sat in our cluttered living room a few hours later, me mentally spiraling around the edge of our relationship drain as I attempted to figure out how I could fix it, him exhausted by the fact that I was having any sort of emotional response about the separation. The cats ignored our obviously painful situation, and Inga, being the oldest of the three and the designated food informant, loudly demanded that we fill their food bowls because they were half-empty, and that's *simply unacceptable, humans*. But cats are selfish assholes and refuse to acknowledge hysterically escalating crises, so I did my best to ignore them and instead racked my brain, trying to figure out why this was happening. What needed to be done next? How could this clusterfuck of a relationship be fixed? After closing my eyes and reopening them a dozen times in hopes that the solution would manifest itself in front of me, I finally connected a few simplistic dots. My body had changed! This was the obvious issue as 1) I had gained weight over the last couple years; 2) he had stopped having sex with me; and 3) he'd said, "I wouldn't be with anyone I didn't find attractive, okay?" one too many times.

I hated to vocalize it, but there was no way around it. "Is this because of my body? Is this because you're not attracted to me anymore?" He shifted uncomfortably on our dingy white Ikea couch and through tight lips said, "I can't say yes or no to that."

All of my insides sank in one swift motion. I knew it. I was afraid of this. I've been afraid of this my entire life, and here was my nightmare coming true, and it was just as horrible as I had imagined. I knew what *I can't say* meant. He knew what *I can't say* meant. Worthless. A complete failure, especially when it came to my body.

Luckily for me, I occasionally find silver linings even in crisis, and this was one of those times. I redirected my thoughts—*This is great! Now I know what's wrong and I can rectify it!* So, I guess by silver linings I really mean a chance to invest in delusions so that I don't have to face the actual issues. I'm great at this. I sat on the opposite side of the sofa, face in my hands—puffy and soaked with tears—my brain working itself into a frenzy while it tried to find a solution to this nightmarish of a situation. I knew I could find one, and eventually I lifted my head. *I know what to do. I'll just work even harder to lose weight! If I can become like I was when we started dating* everything will be fine *again! I will eat more wafers and less real food. I'll get up earlier and go running before the day starts. I'll take those Fen-Phen capsules and work on becoming addicted to kale. This will absolutely fix his emotional incapacities, and we will live happily ever after!*

Oh, Lord, did I need a hug right then.

After I vocalized this brilliant and foolproof decision, he didn't respond. He sat in silence with an emotionless face, unwilling to agree. Meanwhile, I was feeling like I had just solved the world's longest math problem. And I'm *terrible* at math, so this was exciting. This was phenomenal! It would be like going back in time *without* having to build a time machine (ten points for efficiency!), and it would come with a bonus round of food deprivation! Sounds real healthy and rock solid, Jes. Keep that unrealistic shit up.

I'm still not certain what changed my thinking after offering up that quick-fix gem. Maybe it was the fact that I had been writing a body-positive blog for a year and the messages were slowly sinking in. Maybe it was the years of therapy finally catching up with me. Or maybe it was his flat affect and the blatant "I just don't care" vibe that emanated from his entire body. Regardless, my rational self slowly started to take control. I pushed myself into the corner of the couch furthest from him. *No. No, this is not how this works. This is not how love works. You don't conditionally accept someone's body if you love all of them. This isn't about me, and I'm not going to purge myself to the point of misery to try to save the unsalvageable. This is not love at all.* Logical Jes is a little bit of a badass, I've got to say.

Things didn't end smoothly. His mom loved me and begged him to stay. He vindictively left all of his belongings (including an obnoxious amount of worthless football paraphernalia—I now hate the Steelers), changed his phone number, closed my front door the day following our discussion, and I never saw him again.

I cried for a month. I was sure happiness would never be attainable again. I walked around my one-bedroom home that was once too small for two people but now felt enormously hollow with just one. I moped around in pajamas when home, went to school just enough to not be withdrawn, made small efforts when at work, and probably updated my Facebook with one too many heartbroken status updates. Actually, I *know* I did, because my friends quickly threw me a "You're Gonna Make It!" party, partially to celebrate my separation from the dude they apparently never liked, partially to remind me that I was loved, but mostly to give me wine. I wasn't a wine drinker before that party. I haven't stopped drinking wine since. Best. Gift. Ever.

My heart slowly healed, as it always does (and always will). A month and a half later, I posted one of the shortest blog posts I've written to date. It included a picture of me dancing in my kitchen, easel front and center, paper butterflies on the wall. The title was "Whatever Is, To Be," and the text was as follows:

I live alone and dance with my cats. I drink coffee for breakfast and wine for dinner. I skip class but maintain an A. I date 6 people at the same time, all for different reasons. I contemplate karaoke. I contemplate everything. I schedule lady dates all weekend long. I turn up the music I love and make no apologies. I prioritize art above all else. I play the guitar like I invented it. I make family the center of my universe. I fall head over heels in love with bike riding. Again. I remember who I am and what I love. I allow whatever is, to be. I embrace my inner chaos because this is now, and now is good. And later will be even better.

I also blared a lot of Kelly Clarkson and Jill Scott.

This part of my life was like the tired chick-lit narrative of "Girl Goes Through Breakup and Ends Up Falling in Love . . . with Herself." As much as I hate to admit that I'm a living cliché, it happened, and I thank God that it did. I didn't learn to love myself 100 percent (I'm still working on that and probably will be for the rest of my life[3]), but I managed to reclaim much of what was mine in life during a time when nothing good was supposed to happen.

A year and a half later, I invited a boy named Andy who loves John Coltrane and dark green corduroy blazers back to that same (now far less hollow-feeling) apartment. I didn't know at the time that a few years later he would be helping me catch my cats after they made their daily dash into the front yard, cooking delicious meals in our tiny kitchen, and eventually pulling out a vintage engagement ring from his shirt pocket while on his knees. I certainly didn't anticipate spending the last five years together, gifting me half a decade's worth of content about our relationship that I would shamelessly detail in this book.[4] I just knew that his beard made strange parts of my body tingle, that his terrible jokes made me laugh until I snorted, and that he thought it was adorable that I snorted when I laughed. Unaware of this future (and convinced that I was not going to ever see him again), for the first time ever I left my body-image baggage outside the bedroom door and said *Fuck it. I'm going to pretend like I know what I'm doing.* That, combined with an extraordinary amount

---

3. Thanks to a culture that takes our self-esteem from us, waters it down, and sells it back to us at a premium. Cheers, world!

4. The poor guy.

of comfort and his sense of humor . . . well, I rode like a fat cowgirl who's been riding her entire life.

I kid.

It was far from perfect, but I didn't care. I conquered the world that night. The World, also known as Years of Unnecessary Shame.

The lights stayed on. The happiness was real. No trauma. No crushed organs. No shame. And no ambulance was called.

CHAPTER 6

Landwhale

PEOPLE HAVE BEEN hurling animal names at me as insults since elementary school. I'm now thirty-one, and grown adults (sometimes twice my age) somehow *still* find sadistic delight in labeling me as whatever creature they find offensive. Occasionally, people make covert pig noises when I pass them on the street, but most often it happens through short comments from complete strangers on the internet who type very little besides "You're a fill-in-the-blank animal" or, if they're in a hurry, simply an animal emoji. These usually inspire a delete-and-block, though others I leave up for comedic value.

I have a few theories as to why bullies have remained so uncreative over the years and still resort to using animal comparisons and insults. They are as follows:

1) We're all impressively educated when it comes to animal names and noises thanks to the invention of Fisher-Price's lever-pulling "Farmer See 'n Say" wheel. This preschool tool helped us learn not only the names of animals but also

their distinctive sounds, which repeated with one pull of a plastic handle if you needed a reminder. Every toddler who owned one of these inevitably became a bona fide expert in farm animals, and I surmise that regurgitating these things learned as a child is some way of reinforcing how scholastically superior this person was at the burgeoning age of two.

2) The most elementary way to dehumanize another person is to directly compare them to a nonhuman. And while we don't yet know the exact number of animal species on this planet, the list is rapidly approaching over one and a half million, with ten thousand more discovered yearly. This gives snotty kids (the term my grandma uses to address anyone with a severe attitude problem, regardless of their age, which seems appropriate here) a significant list to choose from. Scientists project that someday we might find over fifty million different kinds of animal species living on this planet. That's a hell of a list to choose from.

3) Some adults simply never grow up.

Regardless, as a person living in a fat body for a significant part of my life, being called by the name of or being followed by the sound of a semi-random mammal has become a consistent part of my life, as de rigueur as stopping at red lights, hitting the snooze button seven times every morning, and wondering why Channing Tatum isn't starring in every movie made after he appeared in *Magic Mike XXL*. This, combined with the recent years during which I've actively worked on the internet, has made the verbal abuse so commonplace that it has become less of a slap in the face and more of an annoying buzz near my ears.

Attempting to insult me by comparing me to an animal is one of the rare forms of internet mockery that I find comical. It's a poorly wielded attempt to shame me by drawing attention to the fact that I am fat, which tells me nothing that I'm not already aware of. I'm fat. Got it. And?

The comparison of my body to other creatures, to be totally honest, can be easily reframed as a lighthearted compliment.

Here is an incomplete but satisfactory selection of animal names I've been called:

Cow

See: commonly used Fat Cow derivative.

Cows not only form significant bovine-y BFF relationships but also are brilliant, able to think critically, and capable of solving problems based on past experiences. They love a challenge and are known to jump in the air in celebration after completing a demanding task. Google this shit; I'm totally impressed and definitely not kidding.

Someday I will rock a cow costume for Halloween. I have a bucket list written in cursive, and this is on it.

Pig

See also: Hamhock, Piggy, Fat Pig,
Disgusting Pig, Wilbur, Oinker, etc.

I wanted a pet pig for *years* until I learned what overqualified escape artists they are and how easily they can outsmart humans. I realized that owning one would have just ended up in an embarrassing incident that included me running around downtown Tucson, desperate and panting while asking anyone and everyone if they had seen an escaped pig trotting around the neighborhood that responded to the name Wiggles. If we're going to be real, I was too busy being an irresponsible hipster to find time for runaway-pig shenanigans anyways. In short: they are smart AF.

Call me a pig and I'll not only thank you but take a bow.

Hippo

It feels like it's more offensive to call a hippo a human, to be completely honest. They can easily and happily crush a human skull with their teeth, so perhaps you shouldn't say it to their face. Or do. Whatever. I'm not your mother.

Obese Frog

I tried my damnedest to find *anything* about obese frogs online but failed to find proof they exist. Perhaps the insult was referencing a bullfrog? Even still, I'm pretty sure uncommonly super fat amphibians are not a thing. Frogs are weird (I respect weird), and that, combined with the fact that I've been called something that doesn't exist, leaves me with no option but to award ten points and a high-five to the Reddit community for their (#1 Troll rule-breaking) originality. *Well done!*

Elephant

Everyone knows elephants are basically the coolest animals ever. Try again.

Sea Cow

Also known in real life as a manatee.

I've only had one chance to see a manatee face-to-face (I almost cried out of amazement at the beauty found within the animal kingdom), and I could hardly believe how enormous this creature was. Have you ever seen one in real life? They are *gargantuan*. They can weigh up to two thousand pounds and *they give hugs*. They are the weird-looking social-work mermaids of the sea, and as a weird-looking social worker who's desperately wanted to be Ariel since she was six, I'm so here for it. They are majestic as fuck.

It's a goddamn honor to be associated with a manatee, y'hear me? *An honor.*

Brontosaurus

People have *got* to know that dinosaurs are fucking awesome in every way, right? Add to that obvious fact that Brontosaurus translates into "thunder lizard" and I rest my "How amazing is that?" case.

Land Whale

See also: Landwhale, Beluga, Orca, Shamu, Free Willy,
Beached Whale, Whale, or simply the whale emoji.

Can we just talk for a moment about how the Blue Whale is not only the largest animal to ever exist on Earth (that's eternal MVP status, my friend) but can also vocalize louder than a jet, to the point where human ears can't handle it? Whales also effortlessly jump out of the ocean, mimic human speech, communicate through song, have midwife circles when a new baby is born, and basically run the ocean.[5]

Huge, loud, communicative, singing, leaping bosses of the sea with a supportive community? I see no difference between us. *Nailed it, guys.*

Not to mention that a narwhal (which interestingly seems to get left off the insult list though it most certainly is in the whale family) is basically an underwater unicorn. Imagining one on the beach as a "land whale" posing in a polka-dot bathing suit brings me inexplicable joy and may or may not have inspired this cover.

....

5. There's a rumor that they also have the best sex life out of all mammals. Three is company for North Atlantic right whales!

If I'm going to be completely forthright, the most worrisome comments I could read from these folks would be along the lines of "Jes Baker is a relatable and respectable contributor who fights for an admirable cause. Damn, do we need more people like her!"

The second a fatphobic, misogynistic asshole identifies with and appreciates me is the second I have truly failed this world.

Until then, call me whatever animal you'd like. I quite prefer it that way.

Or, you could just save your breath and start by calling me Your Majesty. We're all grown-ups here.

CHAPTER 7

Things I Thought
I Couldn't Do but Then Did

Tell me I can't do something, and I'll not only try it but also take copious amounts of pictures while I'm at it.

Go skydiving.

There's a strict weight limit for those who want to skydive. And then there is a strict weight limit for fat people who want to skydive beyond that limit, which is, well, pretty damn limited.

If you're fat and want to fall out of the sky, you're forced to step on a scale in front of everyone in line at the skydiving spot (including the apologetic older female cashier who doesn't want to do this either) to see if you make it within the "normal person" weight limit. After driving several hours outside of Tucson, I was fully committed to trying this treacherous adventure, even though I knew I wouldn't make the nonfat cut. And, sure enough, I was right. I was too fat to fall for the normal price. So, I paid the fat tax, aka the extra amount that *only* fat people pay to skydive. I'm still not entirely sure why they do this, but it never occurred to me at the time that this was strange.

Death was starting to feel like an imminent possibility given that I was about to leap out of an airplane that was cruising thirteen thousand miles above the ground, so I called my current boyfriend from the locker room to dramatically remind him that I loved him (for what could possibly be the last time) and harnessed up, the straps pressing my Iron Maiden tee and cutoffs against my body with incredible strength. (No, my outfit wasn't ironic—I was an Iron Maiden fan because they are fucking incredible, obviously.[1])

While the training that day focused on the part where you glide effortlessly with the parachute open, there is one part of the experience that they "forget" to detail in their instructional videos. You free-fall for a few thousand feet first, and gravity is so committed to giving you the full experience that the wind rushes over your ears so quickly you are completely unable to hear yourself screaming with every ounce of unexpected terror you can muster.

This happens for everyone, by the way, in case you're wondering if it's a fat thing. Obviously, because of physics I'm sure I plummeted a tiny bit faster than smaller bodies, which indubitably added to the thrill factor. Perhaps that's what I was paying extra for?

I still resent the *Introduction to Skydiving* video for only showing the parts where you glide like a goddamn pelican until you softball slide into a landing (which I nailed—thank for the years of playing shortstop, Tucson Cyclones!), leaving out the part where your internal organs jump into your throat as you hurtle a million miles per hour toward the ground.

....

1. I mean, kinda, but mostly because my boyfriend loved Iron Maiden and at the time I was out to prove I was not only a hardcore badass, but also an insufferably codependent girl who didn't really know who she was. This non-identity identity was a raging success for quite a few years.

But even so, it was the most euphoric adrenaline rush, and though it has not cured me of my fear of heights (I'm still terrified to climb a ladder), it was worth every penny.

After I initially wrote this chapter, I couldn't stand not knowing why fat people get charged extra, so I looked it up and learned a few things about fat people falling in a professional environment. There is an official weight limit on the glider and straps, so if you're bigger they have to balance your weight with a smaller instructor. Hence, they can't go over a certain amount unless your instructor weighs fifty pounds or is a five-year-old who weighs the same. Nothing about fat tax, though.

Conspiracy theories: 1) They pay their smaller instructors more because they have to fall with horrifyingly fat people and need to compensate for the emotional pain and suffering; 2) They want to encourage you to lose weight, so they give you a discount if you make it under their weight rules;[2] or 3) They like the idea of a fat tax, and because they can get away with it, they do.

So, it's still an unknown, but had I not gained weight since and failed to win the lottery (plummeting from thirteen thousand feet—especially when you're far from thin—is hella expensive), there's a damn good chance I would jump out of a plane every day for the rest of my life.

Come to terms with the fact that I probably have a Tetraodontidae crotch.

The year I turned twenty-two, I spent every waking moment with a group of queer women whose physical presence was more kaleidoscopic than listening to John Lennon on mushrooms. They were spectacularly uncontrollable, a collection of femmes who loved to

....
2. Actual fact: lots of people feel that the weight limit is great because it rewards weight loss. Lord, help us all.

do burlesque, sleep with each other for revenge, dance to Santigold, scream back at catcallers, and snort coke while wearing winged eyeliner sharper than the broken vodka bottles they smashed to make a point at a party. Of which there were many.

I was just uncool enough to be enthralled and honored to be a part of this hell-raising, party-crashing, beautiful mess of women who somehow shimmered more than sequins, glitter, and twinkle lights combined while dancing underneath the disco ball at our favorite club. I was, in short, hypnotized by their effortless magnetism.

One Fourth of July, we gathered at a house for a BBQ (not out of patriotic pride, but rather as an excuse to drink and gossip). I had been mixing several liquors together in a tiny kitchen and sheepishly smiling at the babe with razor-cut black hair who I was never brave enough to sleep with but who always made me regret this with one wink of her smudged and smoky eyes. Drink in hand, I walked outside and caught the middle of a particularly salty conversation about someone's ex.

"I mean, it's not like I'm missing out on anything, anyways." The tone of disgust was unmistakable. "She definitely had a pufferfish vagina."

I sat down to process this exchange. Though this was the first time I had heard the term, I knew exactly what she meant. No, her ex's vagina did not swell to warn potential predators. Simply put: her mons pubis was too fat to warrant a respectable fuck.

I was a grown adult, and still, for years after this conversation, I wondered if I needed to put my crotch mound on a diet.

At that point I had only slept with one woman, and so my knowledge of what a normal mon pubis was "supposed to look like" was limited to mine, hers, a couple of *Playboy* pictures, and the drawings in *The Joy of Sex* that I stole from my parents when I was sixteen.[3] All

---

3. Most of my education around physical relationships came from the LDS church, and though I spent nearly thirty hours a week with their members, the church made a point to never discuss the diversity of reproductive organs, just that sex was the Devil's favorite perversion.

of this, combined with the fact that I was plus-sized, convinced me that if there was anyone else in the world who would have a puffer-fish vagina, it would be me.

I'm still not convinced that I don't.

I'm just smart enough to not give a damn.

Fat-vagina shaming. It's apparently a thing.

Go snorkeling.

I've essentially been told my entire life that anything that involves using my body to move in a way that achieves something successful is impossible. Enter: snorkeling in Belize.

Having never tried snorkeling before (Sonoran Desert dweller here), my anxiety about not being able to keep up with the group and/or inadvertently drowning myself because I couldn't figure out my mask was beyond profound. So extreme, in fact, that I decided to simply live in denial of my fears until Andy signed us up for a date with the ocean. Refusing to acknowledge the fact that I've internalized the belief that my body would fail me in every way possible, I put on my strappy electric-blue swimsuit,[4] and Andy and I braved the only tour we could find on our last day of vacation—a ride in a tiny, worn, orange metal boat steered by a sun-worn man with long sun-bleached hair named "Ninja" who had been doing this for at least fifty years.

Snorkeling goggles and flippers on, we threw ourselves backward into the Caribbean ocean. I quickly realized that once you swallow your first gulp of salt water, you can then easily breathe through your (justified) panic attack and . . . float. Turns out, fat girls float pretty damn well. Know that once you start swimming and allow yourself to feel the incredible energy of the creatures swimming around you,

....

4. Fat-girl tip: Warm water doesn't require a wetsuit, but cold oceans do. Bring your own if you're planning on snorkeling in cold water and avoid the disappointment that yet another company doesn't carry your size. You're welcome.

you'll never be the same. *Deep Sea* on an Imax screen? It will seem like nothing but a cheap puppet show after swimming among ocean life yourself.

We snorkeled through deep underwater cliffs that dropped into dark blue nothingness, Shark Ray Alley—a grassy, waist-deep area of the Caribbean teeming with giant rays and nurse sharks that swam only a few inches underneath us—and a coral reef that simply disappeared into the vastness of the ocean.

It was more extraordinary than I could have ever imagined, my body allowing me to move with the group, experiencing the thrill of out-swimming moray eels (one followed Andy for a few minutes, his curiosity undoubtedly piqued by Andy's tropical-print shorts), as well as mingling with every other Caribbean fish imaginable.

My only regret was not taking the longer tour that visited the manatees. One day. One day it will happen.

Empowered by the realization that my body was not a hindrance in these situations, I also took a solo trip to Jamaica, and we're headed to the coast of Mexico soon. Joining oceanic life is an otherworldly experience I would have tragically missed if I had given in to the lies I've been fed about my capabilities. My body didn't fail me. It gave me experiences so beautiful there isn't a way to imagine them without simply doing it.

P.S. Don't be a hero if you're going to be out all day. Wear a T-shirt. Also, bring a bucket of Belikin.

Find a partner who loves all of me.

The worst I can say about Andy is that he insists on wearing stylish shoes made out of faux leather, and it's a problem I still don't have a solution for.

I mean, how do you lovingly say, "Hey, your choice in shoes is really sexy and one of the reasons I started dating you because I'm superficial sometimes, but also can you wash your socks once in a while, because if they weren't on the porch right now they would kill every living thing in this house, *including* the tree in the living room that is so determined to survive that it's still green after not being watered for six months?"[5]

If you know how to frame this in an affectionate way, help a girl out, would you?

You know that book by Shel Silverstein called *The Missing Piece Meets the Big O*?[6] It follows the quest of a triangle who spends all of his time looking for his partner: a Pac-Man sort of shape which he could fit into perfectly, the two of them forming a complete circle. If you flip through the pages, you'll watch his trials and errors, and see that he's willing to do *pretty much anything* to stop any Pac-Man guy he could find and ask if he is their missing piece. The answer was almost always the same: "No way, dude." There were a few that he tried to partner with, but they were always ill-fitting, square-shaped, and unable to travel anywhere, or a perfect fit at first until the triangular piece grew and then impeded the two's ability to travel.

One day, though, the Big O rolled by and was, like the many others, asked, "Am I your missing piece?" The Big O shared that he wasn't missing any pieces and suggested that the triangle roll by himself. A laughable scrap of advice for a three-cornered shape, but the Missing Piece gave it a try anyway. He flopped over until his corners started to wear off. He bumped along as his edges started to round out. And, soon enough, he was able to roll right along with the Big O, and they lived happily forever after rolling over countrysides . . . or whatever.

....

5. Actually, there's another thing: he gets *really* resentful when I play Adele's *Hello* eleven times in a row but will listen to Elvis Costello's "music" for hours. This is a legit problem we're still working through.

6. No, not O for orgasm, though I'd probably recommend that book too.

I'm still lumpy. Andy's still bumpy. But we can roll with the best of them, and I never believed that it could happen or that I could maintain a feeling of worthiness to allow this to be a part of my life.

And yet . . . here we are. Still loving. Still moving forward. Still rolling together in perfect synchrony.

Receive my bloodwork results and not die of shame.

I've inaccurately judged my psychiatrist for years.

Looking for a clinical professional who worked with my insubstantial form of insurance was a tough enough task, but the fact that I was fresh out of the worst experience I'd ever had with a behavioral health "professional" meant I was the most cantankerous and desperate consumer on the market. And that was on my best days. The last psychiatrist I'd seen loved to decorate with mandalas, candles, and handspun rugs, a believer that the solution for suicidal ideations was *not* the medication that I'd spent years balancing but rather going outside and hugging a tree. A fucking tree.

My affection for candles and throw rugs aside, I may or may not have left a voicemail telling her that she should not be working with patients who have a serious mental illness when she's obviously only qualified to help balanced yogis achieve enlightenment and that she was *officially fucking fired*.

Word to the wise—don't fuck with a crazy person's meds, man. The chance of it ending well for either party is unlikely.

I found my dubious replacement based on insurance, proximity, and my frantic need for said medication, which was running out. Lacking the luxury of searching for the perfect clinical match, I made the soonest appointment I could with Dr. Burns and then instantly regretted my choice the moment I stepped into his office. A thin, white man in his sixties with small John Lennon glasses sat in a recliner, silently studying me as I guardedly took a seat on his leather couch. One glance around the room made it obvious that I was surrounded by a fancy collection of expensive souvenirs from around the world. Fantastic. An old, privileged, clinical dude with shit tons of money.

I could not imagine a person I had less in common with.

But at that point, it didn't matter. The need for psychotropic meds far outweighed my insatiable need to roll my eyes, and this alone kept me planted in his office, explaining my mental history, which, after years of bouncing around the state's behavioral system,[7] I had memorized. He got it. He was efficient. Five years later, I still show up a few times a year for refills, and he begins each session by chatting with me in the way you might with a friend you haven't had coffee with in a while.

I confessed at one appointment that I was tired of being exhausted every day. I explained my exhaustion and how it was making it difficult for me to be available for those around me. I chalked it up to emotional burnout, a side effect of having too much empathy and giving too much support, but he questioned me. "When was the last time you had your thyroid checked?"

"Mmmm," I stalled, eventually settling on offering the truth. "Maybe never?"

He clicked his pen, pulled out a paper with an alarmingly long list, and started circling things that terrified me even though I had no idea what they were. He gesticulated toward the list while signing the bottom. "I have a feeling that, because of other symptoms, you might have thyroid issues, so why don't you go get some bloodwork done and we can address it? We'll have other basic things tested too—you'll need a full lab report."

Here's what a fat person hears when you say *bloodwork*: "A definite way to prove in black and white that your biggest fears about

---

7. Where apparently no one remembers much or records anything.

your body are definitely fucked up and now you're officially a failure to the human race and all the trolls that diagnosed you with
arbitrary illnesses were right and now you can't deny it. Fat person,
just spare yourself the humiliation, burn the paper, and disappear
forever."

I nodded, internally horrified. I was aware that this was important. I was not only tired, but tired of being tired, so I resolved to take
care of this goddamn exhaustion once and for all. And then I lost the
sheet of paper. Twice.

I'm sure it was an honest accident, the list likely swallowed by
my backseat full of random papers, receipts, food wrappers, empty
coffee cups, and cat-litter bags. I searched for it, though. Kind of.
Twice. Kind of. But the searches yielded nothing; I officially had lost
it. My subconscious had apparently decided for me that we weren't
going anywhere near that blood-collecting, morally-damning needle
clinic. And I can't say I blamed it.

After my paperwork disappeared for the second time, I went
back for a third copy, filled with shame around my apparent incom-
petence when it came to holding on to a piece of paper. "I think I
subconsciously am scared to have my blood taken, so I lost the test
sheet. Again," I mumbled, hoping that if I seemed apologetic he
wouldn't sigh out of frustration. He didn't, but instead nonjudgmen-
tally circled what was now the *third* piece of paper and handed it to
me with a smile. The moment I got into my car I hid it from my subconscious (that sketchy bitch) inside of my glove box so no matter
where I went, I couldn't use the excuse that I didn't have it.

A few weeks later, I finally showed up to the clinic. I sat in the
lab's waiting room, eventually moving to the vinyl throne in the
exam room, feeling just as much anxiety as I did when the test was
first suggested. I was stabbed several times for several vials. I waited
the three to five days and made an immediate appointment to hear
the results from Dr. Burns.

JUST KIDDING. I put it off for a month until I was forced to visit him for other medication refills and had no choice but to face the results.

"You're hard to get a hold of." He looked over his glasses at me while I squeezed my hands together, bracing myself for the scolding. "Your physical mail came back, and you don't even have voicemail set up."

"Well, as a millennial, I feel it's my job to ignore the concept of voicemail until it disappears completely."

He didn't laugh. He was always shocked by my experiences on-line when he inquired about them, so maybe he didn't know what a millennial was? So, he didn't find me funny. Whatever, I could handle that. Turning toward his desk, he pulled out a stack of papers and handed half of them to me. "Well, I'm glad you're here. Would you like to go over the results?"

I was far from glad, no; I really didn't want to, and this was something I was unsure I could handle.

The bizarre thing is that, no matter what, I am fully aware that I would *never* walk into a doctor's office and hear, "You're perfectly healthy! Go forth and celebrate!"

I attempted to drown my liver in alcohol for years and started smoking hookah to stave off late-night cravings (heads-up: a hookah diet is *not* a thing). While the smoke-filled food replacement didn't work for shit, it did become one part of a mentally soothing routine that I still utilize every night. But for some reason those things, which are inarguably toxins and tar, don't fill me with shame like an invisible diagnosis that could potentially be blamed on weight.

And for this reason, I haven't had my bloodwork assessed in over five years . . . until now.

Deep breath. "Okay. I'm ready."

Sucking in as much air as I could to prepare for the worst, I picked up my copy and pretended to read along as he rattled off a million numbers and explained what they meant. Yes, in fact, my thyroid was completely out of whack . . . along with other things. Thyroid medication was prescribed, along with a visit to my PCP. I nodded, thanked him, and left the building . . . alive.

I didn't die of shame as anticipated. I hadn't passed out while we went over the numbers. I did go through a complete emotional swing while driving home, though. It ranged from *Holy shit, I'm going to need a gym membership today and to throw out everything in my fridge and replace it with diet food* and was then followed by a *Fuck it all, no one's going to dictate my life. I'm not going to listen to any of this bullshit.* I eventually ended on *I think I'll stop having a panic attack and talk to my dietician during our appointment tomorrow.*

Still breathing, cognizant, and with my self-esteem somewhat intact, I did just that. I didn't lose the stack of test results. I didn't let it define my self-worth. I now have all of the information I need to proceed if and when I'm ready. I'm far from being consumed with shame and am currently feeling like a proficient and legit adult.

Certainly didn't see that one coming.

Wear anything I damn well please.

Sometimes Tumblr comes through and punches you in the face with truth you didn't know you needed to hear.

> "Fuck the idea that fat girls are only seen as hot when they
> have makeup on and a sultry expression on their face like
> the level of femininity fat girls have to perform to not be
> seen as ugly is phenomenal."

Oftentimes "Good Fatty" is a term thrown around to describe a fat person who is intent on convincing the public that they are indeed healthy, or at least working on it. And the incentive to prove that they are "a work in progress" is understandable; fat people who publicly declare their refusal to diet are chased with metaphorical pitchforks.

Until a few years ago, I didn't realize that I was performing another "Good Fatty" role through the way I chose to dress.

In my early twenties, I was dedicated to dressing in pinup rockabilly wear or in impeccable vintage dresses and makeup, never leaving the house without looking "pulled together," often using my makeup, hair, and clothing as a form of ultrafeminine penance for having a fat body.

It makes perfect sense that because many fat women are desexualized, undesirable, and perceived as lazy in every way we would attempt to prove all of those things wrong by performing the most obvious form of desirability a woman can: turning ourselves into sex objects.

This helps us hold on to the currency that we are still *trying*. We *know* we're fat, but look at our attempts to fit your mold anyway! Do we fall on the right side of "good enough" yet?

The answer, until we change our cultural perceptions about fat bodies, will always be no.

Perhaps a few congratulatory remarks will be thrown our way, societal treats to keep us performing. But still, the ultimate answer is no, fat bodies will never be good enough, no matter the outfit, until we, collectively as a culture, unlearn our bias.

I'll always remember the look on my aunt's face as I walked through the door on Christmas last year. Instead of my normal long shirt and legging get-up, I came dressed in a vintage outfit complete with pin curls, perfect eyeliner, pearl earrings, and T-strap heels. Her eyes showed a mixture of surprise, admiration, and disbelief. The amazement reflected on her face at my coordinated and somewhat socially acceptable appearance when I walked in was all I needed to be reminded that I've long since given up on the daily performance of being "pretty." I would use the word *beautiful*, but I feel like that word can mean a variety of things—the Caribbean ocean is beautiful, the way my cats cuddle together is beautiful, human compassion is beautiful. *Pretty*, though? *Pretty* is a definition all feminine bodies are encouraged to embody, something that is a silent pledge we make by doing everything we can to exude sexiness. "I solemnly swear that I am trying to be the best version of me that you require, even if that will never be enough."

And it's never enough.

All we need to do is watch a Super Bowl halftime performed by a thin white superstar and then read the comments online that proclaim her less-than-taut body is an international calamity. But the reality is that in this world, a thin white superstar has more of a choice when it comes to presenting as acceptable. Any thin celebrity leaving her house in a T-shirt with a messy bun is likely to receive far less criticism than will an unknown fat woman in a crop top who is standing in line at Walmart. Social media and website forums have proven this over and over again.

As fat women, we make a decision every single time we post pictures of ourselves, walk out the door, or show our bodies in any way. We can choose comfortable clothing and little preparation with more mockery, or we can choose a polished outfit with the recommended makeup and hairstyle and receive less mockery.

Either way, there will be mockery.

Either way, we're considered a social abomination.

Either way, we will never be "enough."

Either way, according to them, we lose.

I, for one, now choose to be comfortable more often than not, knowing perfectly well that I'm making a mental sacrifice as I face implied (and sometimes spoken) judgment for a physical convenience that I enjoy. I despise rings and necklaces, prefer leggings to slacks, and style my hair up in bobby pins rather than curled—and dammit if I don't love my five dollar ballet flats. My personal comfort and ability to roam the world have at long last become my top priorities. And while I still love to occasionally rock my signature winged eyeliner, a red lip, and polka dots, I remain aware that in order to find personal liberation this must be a choice I make for me—not one that is dictated by others.

I'm aware that no matter what I wear, it will never be enough. I'm aware that, because I currently live in an overwhelmingly fatphobic culture, regardless of how dressy or dressed down my appearance is, I will never win.

And it has finally become clear to me that if I'm going to inevitably lose, I'm going to be as comfortable as I damn well please while doing it.

CHAPTER 8

HAES, Hot Mics, and Other Things I Learned About the Hard Way

HI, MY NAME is Jes Baker. I'm an internationally known body-image advocate. I also haven't exercised in over a year, and I have no idea how to feed myself. I know of *maybe* twenty-five people in the entire world who wouldn't faint in horror at that revelation, immediately condemning me as a complete moral failure. Actually, twenty-six. I'll count myself in that too.

Sure, I've inserted food into my mouth and bicycled around for transportation, but when it comes down to it, I have no idea how to truly listen to my body when it tells me what food and movement it needs.

As someone who publicly challenges diet culture and its harmful effects, I often advocate for the core values of a scientifically-backed alternative approach to nutrition, movement, and overall "health," one that avoids assigning blame around the reasons for someone's weight (because, in reality, some of the reasons I'm fat are completely in my control, and some aren't). It's a concept called Health at Every Size™ (HAES). It preaches the importance of respect, awareness, and compassionate self-care through alternative methods. It

- celebrates body diversity;

- honors differences in size, age, race, ethnicity, gender, disability, sexual orientation, religion, class, and other human attributes;

- challenges scientific and cultural assumptions;

- values body knowledge and people's lived experiences;

- encourages finding the joy in moving one's body and being physically active;

- and emphasizes eating in a flexible and attuned manner that values pleasure and honors internal cues of hunger, satiety, and appetite while respecting the social conditions that frame eating options.

I often summarize HAES as "Treating your body well because you love it, not because you want to change it," and I'm so into it. When first learning about it, I was ecstatic. FINALLY! Something to replace the fucked-up way I've been treating my body! Another way to approach food! The answer to my hatred for the gym! Everything I needed to become healed! And, I thought, if I were to apply this more holistic approach aaaaaand lose weight? That wouldn't be the worst thing in the world, would it?[1]

I read about it. Wrote about it. Taught it. Believed it. Hallelujah-ed it every day to everyone. Read and learned and read and learned. But what I failed to realize is that there is a huge difference

....

1. I know I'm not the only one who has pretended that they didn't pray for this "accidental" outcome. Don't judge.

between understanding concepts and actually implementing them in your life.

A huge difference.

A few years ago, I was contacted by the BBC to participate in a debate with someone who had an "alternative" belief about fat acceptance. After participating in several positive *World News* interviews, I was sure that the BBC was God's gift to America[2]—the interview opportunity seemed like a fantastic idea.

Andy warned me it was likely to be BBC's radio version of a reality show, but I ignored his advice (for the first and last time ever) and enthusiastically signed on. I was debate team captain in high school, and we *never* lost a debate. Nothing could go wrong.

My counter partner turned out to be a woman who had made a name for herself as a Professional Fat Hater from her living room in New York City. I think the title she preferred was Anti-Obesity Advocate or something; I don't remember or care. She hated fat people. A lot.

I researched her before the interview, learning that she had made several noteworthy headlines over the years. One of my personal favorites was her bandit run at a YMCA ice cream social, where she stole the sprinkles from the kids' table and ran off with them all in the name of saving their future.[3] In short, she was famous for that debacle, her animosity, and dramatic sound bites. She was a professional hater, and I was an amateur body advocate with a lot of enthusiasm for body liberation and an inappropriate amount of hubris.

Needless to say, it was a miserable radio interview.

I was wholly unprepared not only for her venom, but also for a recorded debate in which I needed to argue my point in an informed

....

2. Followed closely by *This American Life* on NPR, which, to be honest, would be first on my list if Ira Glass had a British accent.

3. Possibly other toppings too? I would assume that if you're going to take the time to rob children of dessert, you would want to be as effective as possible.

and convincing way. I wanted to believe that I was unwaveringly educated on the subject, when in reality I was intellectually and theoretically miles behind where I thought I was.

I made a complete fool of myself.

Moments after it ended, I turned to the recording engineer in the other room in disbelief, asking her if she heard it all. She nodded, and I used a couple offensive expletives to describe the temperament of this woman I had forced myself to be polite to while on air.

I very quickly learned what a hot mic was.

I put the headphones back on for a commemorative picture (#BloggerLyfe!⁴) when I heard my debate partner's high-pitched tantrum on the other side. Everyone had heard. She was furious, demanding that my vulgar comment be included in the segment and decrying my identity as a feminist.

I froze with my hands on the headphones, unable to move. I eventually managed to numbly remove the earpiece and mouth *OH MY GOD* to the local radio recorder. Her wide eyes said it all: *Damn, girl, you fucked up.*

I try to live without regrets (wasted energy, y'know?), but there are no words for how much I wish I could erase that experience from my vault of life memories. I vowed to never again debate on air, pretend to know more than I did, or call someone a name that I wouldn't be willing to say to their face. I cry-heaved the entire way home. It still feels like the most embarrassing and shameful thing I've ever done as a body advocate. World, I am *so* sorry for my spectacular failure that day. You deserve better.

There was, however, a silver lining to this experience.

The interviewer had a pre-decided slant that worked in my favor, as the debate followed the story of a woman who was fat shamed and had it negatively impacted her life. So, while I waited for the

....
4. I just used a hashtag in a book. I'm giving you explicit permission to quit now and get your money back.

"Fat People Are The Absolute Worst" Advocate to explain her long-winded position about how all large people are ruining the world, the BBC representative cut her off and asked me about my thoughts on health.

I brought up the basic HAES concept but was interrupted by my opponent, who scoffed loud enough to stop me midsentence.

"Oh please, if I were to intuitively eat I would be so *fat*," she snapped back. There was no time for a response at the moment, but the reason she felt this way was clear to me: *Of course she has an issue with intuitive eating. Her relationship with food is completely fucked.*

While the two of us are essentially human versions of oil and water, her comment revealed that we have something significant in common. I, too, have thus far been unable to heal my relationship with food. I, too, had no idea how to listen to my body's cues. I, too, while having not been thin since puberty, was significantly larger than I had ever been, and this was in part—like it or not—because I was unable to fully understand how food played a part in my life. I, too, have a relationship with food that is *completely fucked*.

I know we aren't the only two people in the world to find themselves in this position. The thing is, finding balance with food is an essential part of intuitive eating and HAES, but damn if it isn't a tricky thing for all of us to incorporate into our lives.

....

Deb Burgard a brilliant human who works toward educating the world on healing strategies around food, sums up my roller-coaster relationship with food with a simple pendulum analogy. She explains through her work with Health at Every Size that we all start in diet culture, and when we realize what a goddamn con that is, we often swing 180 degrees to the opposite of what we've been living our entire life: Donut Land. I think of it as a beautiful world of Fuck You's, Frosting, and what feels like newfound Freedom. And for someone who has experienced food scarcity their entire life, it *is* freedom. It's a natural and needed way to balance out years of living in the desolate desert known as restriction.

I've been living in Donut Land for years now, and guess what? It's absolutely delicious. It's kinda like a better version of Big Rock Candy Mountain, where you can lounge by milkshake pools, run on beaches made of out macaroni and cheese, and live in a hollowed-out three-tiered cake covered with Nutella ganache. It's an amazing travel destination.

After realizing what diet culture had contributed to my life (nothing good, we'll just leave it at that) and leaving it all behind, I started eating whatever I wanted, whenever I wanted. Nothing was off-limits, and my middle finger was perpetually in the air while I asked myself, "What is it that I would really like to eat tonight?" and then I made it. Guess what? Good food is really, *really* good. And not having guilt or restrictions around it for the first time in what felt like *ever?* I felt a freedom much like the ecstasy that came from buying my first car at sixteen (an eighties Jetta with a *racing stripe*), which not only had a cassette player but also allowed me to drive to any movie theater and watch PG-13 movies without my parents knowing what kind of promiscuity their Mormon daughter was enjoying.[5]

It short, it was bliss. There was nothing in the world I could not have, eat, or order at a restaurant. So, I settled down in Donut Land for a few years, living my best and most delicious, rebellious life.

There is nothing wrong with living in Donut Land. Absolutely nothing. But a few years later, I found myself in a complicated space—both to live in and to describe.

I hesitate to write about what followed, because Donut Land is a wonderful place to exist in. Everyone should feel like they're able to buy a condo there with central air conditioning and spend the

....

5. Answer: Sexy scenes with Renée Zellweger in *Down with Love.* Sorry, Mom.

afternoons on lounge chairs made of puff pastry layers. I wish this experience for anyone who wants it.

That said, even though I was thrilled with my discovery of this new heaven on Earth, I eventually found myself feeling once again like I was out of control. It's a strange sensation, finding freedom after restriction has ruled your life for decades but still feeling like you have no actual power. I was still reacting to outside influences; they were just more indulgent.

I had fooled myself into thinking that, after spending a few years reading about Health at Every Size, incorporating it into my life was something that would just effortlessly happen. Only recently did I realize that implementing balance is a recovery *journey*. It takes a lot of goddamn internal work.

Was I making decisions based on what *I* wanted every day? Sometimes, yes, and it was amazing. But more often than not, my choices were simply reactions to Diet Land, a place I hated and thought I had left behind . . . but that shit lingers.

I wanted to figure out how to find balance, the middle ground that Deb calls Discernment. The full pendulum starts at Diets, swings to the opposite side—Donuts—and then potentially finds a third option in the middle of it all.

I'll be honest: Discernment sounded like a bullshit concept for a while. It seemed like another diet trick, the same old shit repackaged as a "lifestyle change," which I am smart enough to know is still a diet. *Can't pull the wool over these eyes, world. I'm smarter than that.* I felt like there were only two options: to clutch my new location change as hard as possible or to toss the entire concept in the garbage and start dieting again. It never occurred to me that there was a middle place where you could do neither, but instead just observe yourself, trusting your body to explore, to take risks, to accept the fact that you might fall, and to be gentle with the place you currently inhabit.

Maybe there was actually a place of balance? A place of actual autonomy? One void of rigidity? One where I could make space for myself to heal from a position of trust instead of trying to fix myself while rooted in shame? Maybe I had to stop for a moment and realize that I had no idea what I was doing. Perhaps there was more to learn.

As someone who has been talking about these concepts for years (in a public forum, no less), acknowledging to myself that I had no fucking clue how to start actual healing or even that there were layers included in this recovery journey was painful. It felt like failure. Why was it so difficult to integrate it into my life when I understood the concepts so well? I was smart, educated, and committed, so why wasn't I able to simply walk the talk?

I've come to the realization that professionals exist for a reason.

Dana, a friend and non-diet dietitian who created "Be Nourished"— a therapeutic company focused on body trust—was the only person to whom I felt I could bring this tangled web of concepts. I had no idea how to unravel my mental mess, but hoped that she did.

Dana and I have only just started to explore the reasons why I eat secret burritos in my car. Why I still assign more currency to things like pasta and ice cream, still thinking of them as sumptuous "treats" even though I'm not dieting. Why I panic when our fridge starts to become empty. She's helped me see that no matter how far we come in our quest to trust our body, diet culture will always pop up, and *it's okay*. She has given me permission to say, "What's up, diet culture! I see you and am going to put you on the back burner, okay?" She has shared with me the fact that I am probably going to need to do this internal work for the rest of my life.

Perhaps more importantly, though, she has offered me permission to not blame my completely fucked-up relationship with food and movement on myself. To remove the shame and guilt that came with believing I was responsible for my inability to just "get over it."

Getting over all of my baggage around food and exercise is much harder than I ever expected. When your relationship with food and your body has been fucked with since you were a child, swinging the pendulum across is a natural and healthy reaction to food deprivation. I learned that the struggle to find the middle ground was not only normal, but also not my fault.

Microscopic revelations like this felt more profound than anything else I had experienced while working on trying to "trust my body."

I'm not unfamiliar with moving my body. I participated in what feels like every form of exercise available throughout my childhood. A decade of swim team, during which time I set a city record for backstroke and embarrassed myself when forced to do butterfly. Softball, in which I played shortstop like a champ. Ballet and tap when I was young—and was only there for the tutus. Basketball, which I was impressively bad at. I blamed it on the flat balls. It wasn't the flat balls.

When I was thirteen, my mom would drop me off at 6:30 a.m. every weekday morning at church, where I would join my friends' mothers for an hour and a half of step aerobics before school, not realizing how strange it was that I was the only child in the group as concerned about their body as the adults were. Step aerobics was a regularly occurring theme throughout my life. I was forced to participate in cross-country running, something I hated with a passion, so I rebelliously ran as slow as I possibly could during races until someone's father yelled at me as I neared the finish line, "Stop being lazy, girl, and run faster!" I tried tennis, soccer, weight lifting, bicycling, water aerobics, and years of yoga.

And while this sounds like two decades of innocently healthy movement, almost each and every experience was silently framed as punishment for having a large body. I learned at a young age that any sort of exercise was not to be enjoyed, but rather endured. It was the only way to atone for your weight, no matter how old you were.

A few years ago, I thought that I had finally discovered how to move for pleasure after finding an African-inspired dance class taught by my incandescently radiant friend, Jade. It was just what I needed: equal parts joy, nonjudgment, endorphins, and community. I started to connect with my body in a way that I never had before.

I wasn't surprised that I fell in love with Jade's dance class. That freedom came to me again, the room vibrating with live drumming that filled my body with chills and the ability to move in any way that felt good to me . . . it was heaven.

After a year of finding contentment in this safe space, I mentioned to a friend how amazing I felt after internalizing the magic that happened in the dance room. "That's wonderful," she said supportively. "And you look like you're losing weight too!" It was an innocent statement, but that was all it took to recall years of exercise as punishment and firmly place my dance class on that list as well.

Just like that, the joy was gone. The obligation appeared. The guilt for missing a class made itself comfortable in my mind. Dance was no longer enjoyable. It, like every other form of movement, had become an obligation. Just like when I was in Donut Land but was only reacting to Diet Land, my agency was missing from the equation.

I am astounded by how powerful the message I learned as a child can be. A smart adult, still mentally confined by old lessons. Something that no matter how hard I tried, I couldn't shake.

Shame.

It's powerful shit.

Dance now felt like a form of duty, and I was aware enough of the diet and exercise scam to refuse to be controlled by obligation. I decided to not go unless I felt like it was for fun.

I never attended a dance class again.

I decided to try an experiment and told Andy that I was only going to do movement-related things when I truly wanted to. "Don't invite me on bike rides or suggest I go to class, okay? I'm going to go when I feel ready." Probably in a few months, I hypothesized.

It's been a year and six months so far.

There has been movement in my life within that time, but it's been completely disconnected from anything besides practicality. I bicycled for a week around Belize. I snorkeled for hours in the Caribbean. I have sex, and I'm thrilled when my thigh muscles champion lengthy rides on top of my partner. I swim when it's summer in Arizona. I walk everywhere when I visit NYC. I occasionally bicycle to bars. But these are all things that can in no way be related to my accursed history with exercise.

While my relationship with my body (food, hunger, exercise, and movement) remains the most estranged relationship I have to this day, I have begun to notice small shifts as my birthdays fly by. With each year that passes, my body seems to be able to communicate with me a little more. Or perhaps I'm just listening a little more.

It started with my medications. Years ago, it would take me weeks to notice a difference in myself if I didn't take them. I now notice a distinct difference within three days. Booze was my next internal conversation, my body making it clear that if I didn't want to suffer through hangover hell and Drinking Depression I was going to have to stop drinking everything but wine. It didn't stop there, though; my body was soon explaining that I should be limiting my wine consumption as well, showing me that sweet bottles would cause my bones to feel hollow the next day. And our conversations continued. I slowly started to realize that I needed ten hours of sleep instead of the five I had convinced myself I could survive on a decade ago. I noticed that eating steak made me feel like Thor and over-medium eggs made me feel like I had consumed flubber.

It was gradual, this quiet conversation between my body and mind; a series of neutral observations that simply had to do with what felt good and what didn't. None of these revelations have changed my dysfunctional feelings about food or exercise, but they suggested something I never thought I could experience: my brain and body might be able to work in tandem once in a while, just like I had learned through HAES, but without my forcing it.

Diet culture teaches us to quantify our willpower, to check off boxes to prove our dedication, and to stay within certain parameters if we want to succeed. However, this offers no real solution. Instead, I'm learning that we must step into the void without a promise of anything—not a mile marker to pat ourselves on the back for meeting nor a structure from which we can't deviate. But usually we don't want *maybe*. We want a surefire guarantee, whether we are trying to lose weight or learning to love our bodies. The gray area is terrifying. Accepting that intellect should be replaced by intuition is terrifying. Vulnerability is terrifying.

But I hear that it's the best way to heal.

Recently, after realizing that the amount of stress I had been feeling over the previous six months was causing destruction that sleep, medication, and therapy were unable to solve, and unsure of what to do next, I looked to the most grounded people I knew. And then I copied them.[6]

Acupuncture was recommended by several of these Smarter Than Me people, so I signed myself up for a session the following morning.

I filled out the form, feeling ridiculous as it gave me a sliding scale to rate my pain, obviously referring to physical ailments. I chewed on my lip and tried to ignore the awkwardness that came with writing "depression" instead of "back pain" and "stress/anxiety" instead of "headaches." My scales were filled out honestly; the numbers

---

6. When in doubt, find people smarter than you and do whatever they do. This is solid advice.

ranged from painless to excruciating. One to ten respectively. I momentarily contemplated rating my symptoms at a thirteen.

I walked into a dim room that had meditative music playing softly in the background and a dozen recliners covered with comfortable blankets lining the room in a circle.

After I put my shoes, keys, and phone into the basket next to me, Larry (whose hair and patience were both longer than mine) rolled up and said in a half-whisper, "I looked at your chart. Let's release some of that stress and depression, shall we?"

As he lightly tapped a couple dozen needles into my feet, legs, shoulder, hands, and scalp, we quietly chatted about how his friend was writing a book about climate change. I was so relaxed, everything was interesting at that point.

"So, I'll let you cook here for a little bit until you're done, or I can come get you in forty?" I laid back, determined to soften my face, relax my body, and breathe deeply, enjoying the quietest room I had been to in a long time.

"Hey, Jes?" My eyes shot open. I had fallen asleep. How long had all these strangers listened to me snore? "It's been about fifty minutes; would you like to stay a little longer?" Knowing there was a 180 percent chance that I had been shaking the walls with my obstructed breathing I shook my head. He calmly removed the needles (for those afraid, it doesn't hurt, and if you feel anything you can be sure it's less painful than dry-shaving your legs) and thanked me for coming in. I walked out into the world, noticing how wonderful the sunshine felt for the first time in months.

My legs felt effortless to move. My shoulders seemed to be in a perpetual state of relaxation. My mind was content and calm. There was no walking on clouds—it was definitely a sidewalk—but my existence, for the first time in a long time, no longer felt threatening or painful. Instead, I was blissfully content.

As I got back in my car and closed my door, a great and unexpected revelation dawned on me.

Acupuncture had silently done something that I had been struggling to achieve for years: it had built an infinitesimal but important bridge between my mind and body. For that brief fifty minutes, they touched. They worked together. They healed in tandem.

Mental health? I understand its importance. It has been a priority for me for years after working in the behavioral health field and assisting others through their own mental rehabilitation. I've learned how important it is to create a recovery atmosphere with a team, how to help people rise above the shame that comes with mental needs, and why any focus on taking care of our brain is nothing short of a gift we give ourselves. I knew where I was going. I knew the importance of giving attention to mental health. And I knew how to handle it.

Physical health? I am still sorting out the lies created by medical institutions from the truths my body is trying to tell me. I'm still healing from every form of movement in my life having been a disguised way to lose weight and reinforce that I was a physical disgrace. I'm still trying to differentiate between moving for happiness and exercising to change my body. I'm still unable to mend those enormous broken bridges.

But what I had never realized was that there could be a way to connect the body and mind without my needing to conquer my feelings about exercise first.

Acupuncture accidentally bridged my mind and body. Reiki also bridges my mind and body. Salt water bridges my mind and body. There are so many ways to heal that don't require that we make peace with "exercise" first and I feel hopeful for the first time that eventually these tiny bridges will combine to create an effortless walkway that will lead me toward physical peace. Perhaps there is a world in my future where I could learn how to move within this skin sack of mine in ways that bring me joy.

It's possible, though my future is still full of unknowns. And I'm finally okay with that.

In a world where "healthy is the new skinny" and "health" consistently excludes the mental component, I have reached a point where my decisions need to be based on what is best for me and nothing else. Recovery is not a competition.

Lately, mental health has taken priority over my physical focus, and though I wish I knew how to fully integrate them, I don't. The balance still eludes me. I may not be able to find that beautiful middle way of discernment quite yet, but by accepting the fact that I'm a rad person no matter where I find myself on the pendulum, I have opened a little more space in which I can work toward finding the trust in my body that I lost long ago.

I still have so much to learn, so many books to read, so many voices to listen to. While this is a story about my body, I'm still hesitant to even write about my experiences, however valid they seem. What if there is something obvious that I'm missing? What if the answer lies behind the next paperback cover I open? What if I figure out the be-all and end-all answer after this book is printed, and I'll wish that I could have shared it with you here?

But the reality is that we don't know what we don't know about what we don't yet know . . . and that's kind of the point. I'm going to inevitably look back at this book and sigh, wishing I could rewrite half of this goddamn wordy tome. But this happens to everyone. And while I am positive that as I continue moving forward I will find out more about myself, and also that there will always be—no matter how much work I do or how many years pass—some things that I don't know, I'm simply here to say: it's okay.

It's okay to live in whatever land you need to. It's okay to try something. It's okay to fail at something. It's okay to say yes. It's okay to say no. It's okay to do whatever is best for you. It's okay to swing. It's okay to stay put. It's okay to love something. It's okay to hate something. It's okay to change your mind.

The most important thing I've learned after talking, teaching, and writing about body liberation for five years?

It's okay to not know.

CHAPTER 9

I've Never Owned a Body

MY LIFE. MY RULES.

The words hover above my knees, a reminder—one created by dragging needles across my skin, creating a wound, and then watching it miraculously heal[1]—written in classic script and tattooed years ago by Kristen, a friend who loved cats, hiking, making jewelry, and feathers. All the feathers. I had climbed onto a bench so I could stand while she applied the words in blue with her transfer paper. With the temporary blue outline marking where the tattoo would go, I had sat in her chair for three hours with the buzz of the tattoo gun creating a cathartic hum in the background. This tattoo is unquestionably on my list of the Top 10 Best Decisions I've Made in My Entire Life.[2]

·······························

1. An appropriate metaphor for internal healing as well.

2. Others include dropping out of my university's interior design program midway through before the recession hit (quickly making interior designers a useless frivolity), properly apologizing as an adult to Jaqueline for being such an asshole in middle school (I'm still really sorry, girl), saying "yes" to a Maine Coon kitten when I already had too many pets, and trying oysters once and only once.

Tattoos have been a welcome part of my life since I was twenty, used not only as a way to document my growth but also as a way to reclaim power over my body after feeling like it was never really mine to begin with. They are also a way to decorate and fall in love with the pieces of myself that I've struggled to see. I'm unable to ignore them after they have become art. *My Life. My Rules.* was one of the first times I challenged my history, a history of never feeling like I truly owned my body.

Mormonism, Modesty, and Mastering the Most Amazing Con in the World

"WE ARE DAUGHTERS of our Heavenly Father, who loves us, and we love Him. WE WILL STAND as witnesses of God at all times and in all things, and in all places as we strive to live the Young Women values, which are: **Faith, Divine Nature, Individual Worth, Knowledge, Choice and Accountability, Good Works, and Integrity.**[3]

   "WE BELIEVE as we come to accept and act upon these values, WE WILL BE PREPARED to strengthen home and family, make and keep sacred covenants, receive the ordinances of the temple, and enjoy the blessings of exaltation."

Every Sunday, all the teenage girls would stand and repeat this motto, something we had memorized by heart. It was like the Pledge of Allegiance, but somehow *even weirder.*

For those unfamiliar with Mormonism (properly called the Church of Jesus Christ of Latter-day Saints), here's a crash course in six sentences: If your family loves White Jesus the most, you can live with them in a multitiered heaven forever. Joseph Smith met an angel in the 1800s, then saw God and Jesus in a forest, and they

....
3. Virtue was added to this list years later. Because apparently integrity and accountability weren't restrictive enough to reinforce our obligation to moral purity.

told him to dig up a book made of gold so he could translate it with special glasses made out of two seer stones and then publish it as an addition to the Bible. Each person is a disciple responsible for sharing the homophobic doctrine taught every Sunday with the intent of conversion. You are required to follow the Word of Wisdom (which is very reminiscent of diet culture, by the way). They firmly believe that a man's purpose within the church is to hold the priest-hood (a power Jesus gave to his apostles that has been handed down to current dudes to act in the name of God) and a woman's role is to make babies after marriage, not question why they aren't allowed to also have the special power, and perhaps most important, to remain chaste AF.

Oh, and you're required to give 10 percent of your income to the church and be baptized if you want the perks of being able to enter their earthly temples or make it to the best part of heaven.[4]

If you studied a lineup of Mormon prophets' faces starting from the history of the church to today, it would look almost exactly like the succession of the U.S. presidency. In fact, it would be nearly impossible to tell them apart from a few feet away if it weren't for Barack's face near the end of our whitewashed American leadership list. Prophets, however, not only held earthly positions of power, but also were able to pass moral judgment and determine your eternal fate.

In short: Mormom men not only ran this world, but apparently heaven too. This impacted my life in more ways than I ever expected.

....

No one can argue with the fact that I was an exceptional Mormon. I was baptized in a frilly white dress in the sacred Salt River when I was eight; paid tithing from the moment I had an allowance (I'd love

---

4. They refuse to disclose their finances, but it's a pretty damn lucrative business.

to send the dudes in Salt Lake City an invoice for *that* highway rob-
bery); was asked to be *the* youth camp leader (like, the seventeen-
year-old in charge of all the other high school youth leaders and
younger attendees) for hundreds of girls at our church summer
camp; graduated from seminary (a 6:00 a.m. weekday church near
your high school where you memorized a lot of scriptures and
proved that you loved God more than sleep—it was a big deal); went
to a Mormon university; taught the "Gospel Doctrine" course to
rooms full of college students (they let *this* asshole teach Mormon
history to hundreds of students *weekly* even though one time I tried
to use the *National Treasure* movie as an analogy for the Book of
Mormon so we could just watch it for an hour, and used a pulpit
to talk about the importance of including queerness within our
communities. That's when they started to catch on); prayed multiple times a day; starved (erm, fasted) when required; listened to a
lot of Mormon Tabernacle Choir; prayed for Rachel and Lizz after I
saw them buying coffee at the airport; and even took a legit college
course called "Eternal Marriage." *Three whole credits, baby!*[5]

I was really *good* at being Mormon.

This understandably meant that I internalized a lot of bullshit.
About all kinds of stuff. Such an incredible amount of bullshit that
we could talk about it for hours, but that's what I pay my therapist
for, so we'll cover the one relevant part: I became especially fucked
up about my body.

I had already learned from all media and my father that my body
size was detestable, but the shame didn't stop there. Through the
misogynistic teachings of Sunday School, I also learned that my body
was dangerous. The chastity shit became real as I hit puberty, my body
changing into something that could potentially distract boys, and for
this reason it was made clear that I was to completely cover it up.

....
5. No, they didn't transfer anywhere else.

All teenagers were given an owner's manual for our lives called "The Strength of Youth." This concept detailed in the most straightforward way possible that

> "When you dress immodestly, you send a message that is contrary to your identity as a son or daughter of God. You are also sending the message that you are using your body to get attention and approval."

While this paragraph included "sons" as well as "daughters," the day-to-day reinforcement was clear: it was the women who were responsible for always covering their bodies. Any showing of scandalous skin would inevitably tempt the boys around us, and should they ever give in to their uncontrollable urge to act in a sexual way (or even to have impure thoughts), it would affect their ability to go on a mission (the most important thing a young man can do) and would bar them from Celestial Kingdom.[6] Not only were we responsible for our actions, which had eternal ramifications, but we were also responsible for the influential men as well. It was the woman's duty to save every boy's bright future.[7]

Short skirts, sleeveless tops, tight clothing, revealing dresses, plunging necklines, and suggestive messaging were prohibited at all times.[8]

Convinced that floor-length denim skirts, long-sleeve shirts, and loose clothing were the only way to fulfill my duty, I embraced modesty wholeheartedly. This faulty rule worked for me in more ways than one; because I believed that my body was repulsive, broken, and

....

6. A fancy name for heaven.

7. Which leaves me repulsed by how dangerously close this comes to mirroring rape culture.

8. While at BYU–Idaho, the dress code also banned flip-flops and "unnaturally colored hair." Religious professionalism was required at all times . . . or else.

now dangerous, invisibility seemed like it was for the best. Invisibility made it easier to be good. Invisibility got you into less trouble. Invisibility meant you could focus on important things like finding new spiritual quotes to print onto colored cardstock so your friends could glue them into their already bulging scriptures.

....

Excuse me, ma'am, we're campaigning for Sears to offer more modest clothing options; would you like to sign our petition?

It was summer in Tucson, and I was wearing a three-quarter-sleeve red shirt and below-the-knee floral skirt from Charlotte Russe, its brightly colored print the only noticeable part of my appearance. My cherubic face was makeup-free, framed by my middle-parted blonde hair and accented with a sweet smile only a thirteen-year-old who believed in three kingdoms of heaven could give. This was a normal look for me and also apparently made me an approachable campaigner, as library guest after guest agreed to sign the petition I held out to them.

The rhetoric around "modesty at all times" shared a philosophy with things I saw posted online—*"Dear girls, dressing immodestly is like rolling around in manure. Yes, you'll get attention, but you'll also attract pigs. Sincerely, Real Men"*—and I was all in. After all, clothing that hid my fat teenage body made me feel even more inconspicuous. *Not* that I felt like I was irresistible enough that a boy would lose his place in heaven for me to begin with, but it reduced any microscopic chance that existed. I didn't want to tempt those poor, righteous kids who were unable to control their actions, y'know?

We eventually collected the required number of signatures to send to Sears (it was a lot) and then celebrated with a fashion show that had the motto "Modest Is Hottest." Catchy, yes, but problematic in a million ways. I mean, besides the fact that I wore an ill-fitting and chunky denim skirt and a scarf the width of a bookmark. That was dubious too. Sister Bethany, *why did you let me wear that on a runway?*

Not unlike our culture at large, my body's worth was decided by the men in charge. But instead of being judged on a scale of "fuckable to unfuckable" like it is now, it was judged from "heaven-worthy to hell-worthy."[9]

In college, my body's purpose was finally made clear: be attractive enough (but modestly so) to get married and then birth seven million children so that the church could grow. If the church could grow, you could experience the gift that women could offer the world: new life. Women were not allowed to have God's holy power on Earth to heal things and know all the secrets, but we were reminded that having kids was an even greater gift. We believed it all.

While in college, we were required to attend a weekly event, known as "Tuesday Devotional"—a stadium filled with students who came to hear different, yet always important, LDS speakers share some weekly wisdom. The entire campus shut down for this hour, leaving you no reason to miss each week's message.

We sat in velvet-covered auditorium seats, folding them down to get comfortable and prepare for the upcoming inspirational lecture. I'm unable to recall a single message heard from those seats aside from one Tuesday sermon that I doubt I'll ever forget: a nationally known white-haired leader (male, obvs, because God loves speaking to them *a lot*) who leaned on the pulpit, elbows locked and hands firmly placed on top of the wooden structure, and looked out at the thousands of students in front of him. He started speaking but paused in the middle of the address to speak to the female students in the audience specifically. He instructed us in no uncertain terms that, if given the chance to either start a family or finish college, we should *always* choose the first option. No degree could possibly offer

---

9. We called it Outer Darkness. Again, fancier name.

us the personal fulfillment or happiness that being married to a man and reproducing until we had our own little commune would.

Today, the fact that I am currently an unmarried woman living (in prohibitory sin) with my long-term partner, both of us comfortable in our D.I.N.K.O.P.[10] lifestyle, *yet have still achieved happiness* would likely blow his paradigm to smithereens and ruin his faith in a religion he's monetarily invested 10 percent in since he had an allowance. With that in mind, I sincerely hope he never finds this book; I'd hate to have that personal breakdown on my conscience.

I obviously didn't listen to all the men who explained things to me while I was growing up. If I had, not only would I not be living my D.I.N.K.O.P. life, but I also would still believe that God lived on a planet "humans haven't found yet" called Kolob, that consecrated oil could heal illnesses if a righteous Mormon man blessed it, and other bizarre things that made a person with a penis the master of everyone's universe. But plenty of the messages came through clearly: my body was dangerous, not to be shown or used in any way unless I dropped out of college, got married in one of God's ordained castles, and created as many adorable creatures with opposable thumbs and obvious death wishes as possible.[11] Got it.

....

10. Dual Income, No Kids, Only Pets. *Highly* recommended, if only for the simple fact that it's against the law to lock your kids in crates when you leave home.

11. I once took my red-and-yellow plastic Little Tyke's Cozy Coupe out for a ride on the busy street just outside our apartment complex. I was four years old and convinced that those little rugged tires could keep up with the rest of traffic. Cars belonged on the road. Why wouldn't this apply to mine as well? My mom remembers grabbing me as I patiently waited for the opportunity to make a right turn and laughs at what a "daredevil" I was. I look back and am horrified at what a goddamn liability all children are. (I also liked to swallow pennies so my parents would have to call the firemen to save me. This is how I entertained myself and also is the reason I'll forever be child-free.)

Luckily, my lack of self-esteem and abrasive "Fuck with Me If You Dare" attitude kept all boys at bay. [12] While my friends were getting engaged left and right, I was sledding down snowy hills on cookie sheets, blaring Hilary Duff while throwing magazines against the wall to release anger, crying in the laundry room, and locking the doors so I could watch *Amelie*, which contained a scene with *orgasm noises*. Naughty, naughty, right?

And thus began my decline into inevitable hedonism and atheism, which for me are pretty much the same thing.

The Time I Only Existed for the Male Gaze

I remember the exact moment when the concept of someone finding me attractive became even a remote possibility. Still reeling from living in this invisible and unexplained but clearly weaponized body for my entire life and then leaving those beliefs behind once I left college. I was twenty years old, talking to a friend, when they said with a snicker, "Can you believe Henry thinks you're hot?"

Apparently, Henry was not one to be flattered by. He didn't have girls lining up to date him, and he didn't possess any qualities of what some might call a "good catch," but these details were lost on me. I was shocked and stunned by the fact that *any* homo sapien would find my body attractive.

Growing up, the church's restrictions and constant warnings left me feeling so desexualized that the idea of any sort of physical appreciation was inconceivable. Yet, here I was. A real live human

....

12. It became obvious that defiance is hereditary after finding out that my seventy-year-old grandmother shouted at the Swiss Guard for harassing an older man at the Vatican and then took off running when they tried to confiscate her phone after filming their poor behavior. She attempted this escape after having had a knee replaced, for the record. Badassery also runs in my family.

found me attractive. It was in this moment that my wheels started turning—cue my two-year stint of reckless debauchery.

I really wish I could say that I never stepped foot into the world of endless one-night stands purely motivated by wanting attention on my body. I wish that I grew up thinking that I was enough not only on the inside but on the outside as well. I wish that I was raised to celebrate, love, cherish, and appreciate my body for all of the wonderful things that it does and is, but I wasn't.

I grew up mortal enemies with my body, so much so that I was completely and utterly detached from it. Me and my body were separate entities altogether, fused only by physical proximity. My body was the friend that people tolerated so they could hang out with the rest of me. My poor body. So hated, reviled, ignored, camouflaged, shunned, demoralized, and loathed. My body was neglected and famished for attention, and so I jumped at the chance to be with whoever would have me.

When it comes to self-esteem, I've learned that the way we regard ourselves is based on every interaction we have ever had in our whole lives. If you learned, even subconsciously, that you were not okay, well, my friend, it's an uphill battle for the rest of your life. As Lesley Kinzel says in her book *Two Whole Cakes:*

> "Fat women learn early that they should take male attention wherever they can get it, because what self-respecting man would want to fuck a fat woman? Not only does this knowledge reinforce the idea that fat women do not deserve to be seen, but it also positions fat women as targets for men looking for an easy lay—she'll take what she can get, regardless of what she actually desires, and consider herself lucky. The idea of such a woman saying no is inconceivable."

Fat women are taught that we have failed at something that is unforgivable, and that failure decreases our worth as human beings. We have committed one of the worst sins and should thus be punished, and if we get any attention we should be eternally grateful that the fat gods have smiled down on our pathetic subhuman selves.

I believed it all. Thanks to the shitty self-esteem I accumulated growing up, I was easily seduced, fucked, discarded, and then used as a ladder to get to more attractive (read: worthwhile) girls. All of this would start and end in quick succession, and I had no idea that I should have been bothered by it. After all, I had zero frame of reference for what healthy sexuality might look like, thanks to the church's insistence that it all be kept secret, hidden, and valued only in the context of marriage. I was just amazed (and impressed with myself) that I got so much attention.

I am not concerned about the number of people that I slept with. Grown-ass adults can sleep with as many (or as few) people as they damn well like. This doesn't make me *any* of the crass names that people like to call sexually active women.

But I have to be honest about my intentions.

I was still functioning under the premise that men (usually cisgender white ones, mirroring my experiences in the Mormon church) were the desirability deciders.

I wasn't reclaiming my body; I was trying to fuck my way to the top of the desirability scale. After all, the more sex I had, the closer I was to winning. That was how self-worth worked, right?

But the only person I was fooling was myself. I was letting anyone and everyone take my need to feel sexy and exploit it. I wasn't bestowing anything on anyone; I was allowing myself to be stolen from. I didn't value myself, and therefore the interactions themselves had no value.

I hate thinking about how much I bought-in to this patriarchal scale of worthiness. I deserved better. Better intentions and better care. I wish I would have said "yes" when I wanted yes and "no" when I wanted no. That simple.

After those debaucherous years and the following few wherein I dated a sex addict (sex equals love, right?), I started to understand that I was being duped. When each rendezvous ended, I was left with just as much self-hatred as before. I started to see that physical attention wasn't a cure for self-loathing. I slowly and consciously started to learn how to say yes and how to say no, giving both my psyche and my body the chance to choose what they actually wanted. I started liking myself a little more each day, and eventually I found Andy. With his support, I have been able to dabble with the concept of embracing myself a little more each day.

My body hasn't been on the socially designated "fuckable scale" for a while now, but I no longer feel the need to climb that ladder. I am not here for the men in this world—not as a scapegoat or a baby-maker, and certainly not solely for their sexual satisfaction. My purpose is far greater than shallow bullshit.

Never again, my friends. Never again.

Men Explain How My Body Works

"Okay, I agree that you should love yourself, but you should in fact be worried about . . . hmmmm, heart disease, diabetes, high cholesterol, high blood pressure, and a slew of other issues that come with gaining weight."

Dr. Oz's biggest fan had found one of my body-acceptance posts and decided that I needed to be educated on how my fat body *actually* works and what my current priorities should be. This was followed by an essay that isn't interesting enough to be shared in full, but in summary said something like this: *"Be proactive! Heart disease! Heart disease again! Obesity is synonymous with heart disease! Have you heard about this awful thing heart disease? Love yourself and don't get heart disease! Much love!"*

That is obviously a simplified (but considerably accurate) version of the rest of his advice, but that last sentence, honest to god, was how he signed off. *Much. Love.*

Lord, grant me the patience.

This comment isn't novel, however. Every day I have men attempting to explain to me how bodies work. There are men who attempt to explain how my *female* body works. There are men explaining how all other men know more about me than I do. Men explaining who I am and what I'm worth. Men explaining how not only he but all other men as well can accurately predict my future health, relationship outcome, career successes, and life span. Men who have decided that policing a fat woman's body is a sport—one they are all striving to be the best at. If it weren't so pervasive it might be funnier.

Fat people, if anything, are more likely to be *hyper* aware of every bit of simplified obesity info and statistics already. Most of us have been hearing these warnings since we were in kindergarten. So, the reality is that a *lot* of fat people (even female fatties!) already know an extraordinary amount about "health." We are very familiar with the idea that being fat is "bad" and have likely heard it not only from our aunt, best friend, and maybe doctor but also from the old woman on the subway. Our world is saturated in anti-fat rhetoric, threats, and solutions.

We've been on diets since we were children in the name of health. There is not one single thing you can tell us that we don't already know. We've gone to fat camps, gotten brochures from strangers, had long talks with our concerned parents, received those "helpful" articles about the new study that shows that eating almonds is now a bad thing, and butter *was* a bad thing but now it's a good thing, and raw nuts are actually the best, and you have to exercise for at least thirty minutes a day to not die when you're twenty.

To add to the strangeness of unsolicited advice, I worked in a health-food store for years, where it was my job to be able to tell you exactly what supplements to take for smoking cessation, how to boost your immune system, why you probably don't want that soy protein powder so try this one instead, and which amino acids will totally boost your brain, and yes this is locally grown kale. Oh, and here are some frozen shots of wheatgrass juice—would you like fish oil to go with it? My life for years.

But, yeah, thanks for taking up my time regurgitating things I've known since kindergarten.

We know. We get it. We've heard it. So, I'm so sorry to have to tell you this, but your comment is not only unwelcome and unoriginal but also completely futile.

Could you just leave comments about how a flock of ravens is called a murder instead? How the human body produces enough saliva during its lifetime to fill two swimming pools? How cherophobia is the fear of having fun? How when approached from a botanical standpoint, strawberries and raspberries aren't berries, but bananas and avocados are? Literally *every other fact in the world is more interesting than what you're saying about my body right now. PLEASE TRY HARDER.*

I wrote about my experience with date rape once, years ago, when I was in a naively comfortable place of knowing just enough about the internet to write personal essays and not enough about the internet to know that sharing freely means your stories will unavoidably be misconstrued, reconstructed, and shredded by every single man who wasn't there. They know best, after all.

I deleted the post recently after glimpsing a comment elsewhere about how I'll do anything for attention, even make up a rape story when it couldn't have been true, because we were both drunk[13] (so many internet strangers were apparently there that night; how creepy), and I remembered that while it was posted way back in the archives, it was still there, poorly written with an innocent trust that I no longer have, waiting to be ripped apart by web wolves.

As I removed it, I didn't dare to look at any of the comments that had accumulated over the years. I don't expect they were anything other than scathing comments from men who feel it's their duty to explain exactly what rape culture is to me and how I was once again playing the victim in this great piece of fiction I'd written.

I didn't need that, and I have much better ways to spend my energy, if I'm going to be honest.

Fortunately, one of the opportunities I have includes lecturing at colleges, often receiving lines of people waiting to hug and thank me for my message and wanting to share their personal story and be heard. This intimate interaction, often offering me a brief reprieve from internet tomfoolery, is what I live for.

Unfortunately, mansplainers now love to follow me there to offer their expert opinion on my body as well.

I'm a Fat Liberationist who is unapologetic about health and preaches the belief that people don't owe their health to anyone and being unhealthy is okay. Once I started making the purposeful decision to talk about these topics specifically, I noticed a huge change in the way I was received.

I also started to notice a growing number of people who liked to use the question and answer session not to solicit a query, but instead to lecture me on the thing I had spent five years researching (using decades of other research) and had just discussed for over an hour.

....
13. "It's increasingly clear that for men, being drunk excuses anything they do. For women, being drunk excuses anything done to us." Truth bomb from Louisa Smith, aka God's Gift to Twitter

Last year, after giving an evening lecture in Flagstaff, Arizona, a young, thin, straight-presenting man raised his hand when I asked if there were any questions. The student aide took the microphone to him and stood aside to let him pose his question.

Before asking anything, he dropped the mic to his side and pressed his thumb and pointer finger on the bridge of his nose and closed his eyes to think. We all watched, wondering what was so intense that he needed to regroup while standing in the spotlight.

After speaking so many times and answering so many questions, I assumed he was gathering the details of a personal story he wanted to share or trying to figure out how to explain how complicated it was living as a man in this beauty-obsessed society.

It was neither of those things.

"We have a giant problem. By the year 2030, obesity rates will have increased by . . ."

I stopped listening and just blinked while watching this man who had decided that it was his turn to lecture a fat woman about how fat people and their lack of control are dooming the world. He spoke slowly (so I could understand, I'm sure), as if I had never heard of this calamity called the Obesity Crisis. After pushing aside my disbelief at his blatant display of unoriginal insolence, I eventually refocused myself on Mr. TellMeSomethingIDontKnow to catch the end of his current thought, "I mean, this is a huge issue that affects us all . . ."

I was dumbfounded by the casual tone in which this man felt he could challenge a fat person's worth and Armageddon influence to their face. Was I supposed to laugh? Yell? Explain *again*?

Before I had time to decide what the appropriate response would be, the student leader who was in charge of the event interrupted him: "This is a Q and A. Can we not give a lecture and instead ask the intended question?" Caught off-guard by someone daring to redirect him, he mumbled, "Well, y'know, it's the same as the last question she asked," pointing to the pre-med student who had insinuated that the elimination of harassment and discrimination toward fat people shouldn't be something to concern ourselves with because fat people choose discrimination willingly simply by existing.

I took a deep breath, but they weren't finished.

"Well," Obesity Crisis's friend occupying the chair next to him piped up, "I believe in being happy and loving your body, *but* . . ."

I stopped the comment midsentence.

I smiled and repeated the words back slowly, not for those who were there to challenge the worth of fatties, but for the rest of the auditorium, all of whom were visibly shrinking in their seats as those insensitive statements were being made:

"I. Believe. In. Being. Happy. And. Loving. Your. Body. BUT."

It took everything I had to not verbally decimate them for the entitlement and sheer audacity to spew lazy information in an effort to publicly shut me down. But I promised myself that I would answer this with composure.

I replied by reminding them that it's not as simple as we want it to be. I asked, "If we're going to have a conversation about the obesity crisis, why are we not talking about classism?" Fingers in the back snapped in agreement and relief. "Why aren't we talking about poverty and single parents who have very little control over the food they can purchase and eat because certain things can be frozen or preserved while other food items cannot? Why aren't we talking about food deserts and how many don't have access to fresh food at all? Why aren't we talking about children who grow up in homes where they have no control over their environment, so they feed their bodies—the only thing they have reign over? The main message: the situation is complicated."

Most of the students left, but Obesity Expert and his friend stayed around to talk one-on-one afterward. They appeared to be determined to take up as much space and as much of my time at this lecture as possible. I stood while he sat on the edge of the stage, one leg swinging casually.

"I just feel like you think that being unhealthy is okay," he sighed in annoyance.

"I do," I replied matter-of-factly.

"Well, you said that people should try to become *more* unhealthy," clearly feeling like I wasn't understanding his very important argument.

"No, I never said that."

"Well," he paused, "that's what it sounded like."

They had maxed out my tolerance for manipulation that night. "No, that's what you *heard*. I didn't say anything of the sort; I simply said that health means different things to different people, and they get to decide what works for them."

A blessed but brief moment of silence.

"Well, I just don't agree with Health at Every Size." His desire to repress frustration was starting to unravel; my eyes were aching to roll.

"That's fine. I'm not here for you. I'm here for all of the people who have heard every statistic you spouted already, and then had to hear them again in what is supposed to be a body-positive space, which damaged their security. I'm here to help them heal from people like you who share generalized and dehumanizing judgments as if you're not actually speaking about people who are currently in the room."

He had nothing and decided to switch tactics in a fascinatingly self-implicating way.

"Well, why didn't you talk about bullying?"

I sighed. I was tired. This was ridiculous. "I'd rather give people tools to build up self-confidence than reiterate what we all go through; besides, you did a great job of showing what bullying looks like, whether you knew it or not."

I turned to his friend, "As did you. When you said 'everyone deserves happiness *but*' you were causing most people to try to figure out if they were worthy to fall on that side of the line."

There wasn't much more to say.

The friend mumbled something about how they had family that they tried to help live a healthier lifestyle, but maybe it was just as well to give up and simply support them as humans instead. "Isn't that what it's all about?" They looked to me for validation.

I gathered every generous piece of my soul I had left and found a one-word answer: "Kinda."

They left, clearly unresolved and without any of the applause they felt they deserved for their concern for fat people's health. I felt nothing but gratitude while watching them walk away.

This experience is no anomaly. I had sat through a luncheon at a different university, months earlier, where the room was full of a diverse group of women and a couple male faculty members, one of whom grew increasingly hostile as we talked about body image. He made it known that he used to be fat but through sheer willpower alone had fixed his body. Because of this, everyone else could and should too. He spent the hour interrupting students, dismissing their experiences, and telling the group that if they would simply watch less Kardashians and go on a walk instead, he wouldn't have to be inconvenienced by the medical bills fat bodies rack up that he, a perfect human specimen, must then cover. He abruptly left the room midway through, leaving one student in tears and another professor and I so shaken that we cried later.[14] He, in short, was an incredible asshole.

....

14. He did have the time to attend my lecture, though, and when I asked the audience for an affirmation that they identified with, he was happy to offer his. "Well, I didn't kill anyone today," he said smugly, making sure I was aware that this comment was directed toward me. Class act, this guy. Class act.

Non-fat, hetero-presenting men (often white and surreptitiously bolstered by their participation in academia) still continue to steal from fat, queer, disabled, trans, and/or bodies of color, insisting that they get to be the gatekeepers of who gets to accept their body. That they understand the headlines we're all too familiar with better than we do. That they, and they alone, are the rightful rulers of a safe space that was built to escape their domination in the first place. Because having the rest of the world available to them simply isn't enough; they want our designated areas too, and they'll use our verbiage against us when necessary to convince us that we should be ashamed for being selfish by demanding the right to exist while feeling worthy of respect.

The creepiest thing is often their casually judgmental statements that fat people deserve existential punishment; it's been presented to me as an undeniable fact countless times. I am also left speechless by the fact that our society has taught these people that they, by insisting on humiliation, are doing fat people a favor. That they are doing their civic duty and making the world a better place. Oh, to be so self-righteous while feeling so humble. What a world.

When fat people talk about health, nothing we say (and I watch this happen) is truly heard. And the more weight I gain, the more my message is laughed off. The more they shove me into the "unintelligent fat person" box. The more they decide that I live in denial no matter how much research I have done. It's because of this that I purposefully share concepts of health and then show pictures of the thin nutritionists, researchers, dietitians, and doctors behind them. Audiences, unsurprisingly, take research more seriously when it comes from someone who is slender.

The real-life demand for me to defend myself, on top of the incredible amount of harassment that I receive online, on top of everyday interactions in a world that wishes I didn't exist, does build. It gets difficult. And sometimes it becomes unbearable.

There are certainly days when I just feel like screaming *My body is not here for you. My message is apparently not meant for you. Won't you just let me fucking live?*

But still, I continue to share the message of body liberation. It's needed as much as ever.

....

My body has never been my body.

My rules have never been my rules.

My life has never been my life . . . until now.

And those three reasons are why I continue to love my knee tattoos. The four inked words are the essence of something I have sworn to never forget: my physical appearance was a problem that I spent my life trying to fix, allowing others to dictate the solutions. But the issue was never my body. Instead, the true issue lies in other people's opinions—all intended to strip me of both internal and external freedom.

It doesn't matter how many people have tried to lay claim to, own, or dictate how I use my body in the past. Today, it is very much mine and mine alone.

My body, my rules, my life, motherfucker.

CHAPTER 10

Sick

MY THERAPIST IS UNFLAPPABLE.

I say that after having spent over eight years visiting her office and showing her every side of me that exists. Yelling, crying, laughing, and everything in between. Sharing every unfiltered detail of this roller-coaster of a life for the vast majority of my tumultuous twenties.

This woman has seen *some shit*. And that's not taking into account the decades of shit from other clients she has seen as well.

Yet, she has unfailingly been there for me, showing up week after week in her draping, oversized lagenlook linen blouses and long silver shell necklaces with patience comparable to no one else on Earth that I know. Her "body coherence" is so advanced that no matter what is thrown at her, she can sit and embrace it without its remotely alarming her nervous system. Sure, she's a fallible human in her own right, but even still, the wholeness of her presence reminds me weekly of my ultimate goal: to develop the ability to handle life's loose cannons with the grace of someone whose internal work has healed them on a cellular level. It's obvious to both of us that this goal will take herculean effort, but we're equally invested, even if it takes a lifetime. She continues to appear every Thursday afternoon, reclined in her roller chair in front of me. Engaged, brilliant, compassionate, and assuredly unflappable.

I'm not sure why I expected anything but an unruffled response when I showed her a particular comment thread.

You inevitably learn after working online for half a decade that googling your name is something that only self-flagellating amateurs do. I know this because I was this kind of novice for years, unable to quell my destructive curiosity about what could *possibly* be so horrific about me that people would spend an astonishing amount of time discussing it. After reading innumerable (repetitive) posts dedicated to dissecting your failures, you finally figure out that this quest for proof of how much evil humanity can embody is rarely informative or inspiring. Unfortunately though, even after learning this lesson well and being at the top of my hypervigilance game, I still occasionally and accidentally stumble upon something so emotionally violating that I swear to myself that I will *never* open a browser again, something so horrific that I feel the need to frantically cleanse my house with Florida Water and smudge it with sage so the filthiness of other people's souls that leaked through my screen can no longer linger in my hundred-year-old, charmingly deteriorating, brick-built sanctuary.

While searching for images to use in a post about *radical fatties your life isn't complete without*, I unintentionally stumbled across a thread written about me on a notorious "Fat Hate" site. Momentarily frozen after reading the heading—a local person in Tucson exclaiming that they had been behind me in line at a grocery store that day—I couldn't tear my eyes away from the 108 comments that explicitly dissected my casual errand of shopping at the midtown Trader Joe's.

A local fitness extremist had caught sight of me scandalously

buying wine, fingerling potatoes, and cookies[1] along with other un-
specified food items (there were more, but they were left unlisted so
that a communal gasp could be shared over my receipt total), and apparently this was the most important thing that had happened to her
that day. She ostensibly ran to the internet after returning home to
reassure others that I am indeed as terrible as they have been thinking all along. The comments that followed attacked my body, both
the visible aspects and their own diagnoses of invisible maladies.
Because I didn't invite a doctor to Trader Joe's to hold my health chart
open for the public to read while shopping, those in the forum were
left to freely make their own diagnoses of illnesses that I obviously
had or would eventually get. They all ended up coming to the same
conclusion: I was inevitably going to die.[2]

My character and everything else that could be extraneously
gleaned from standing behind me at the register were documented
in the harshest and most fabricated way possible. Encouragements to
literally gut me while I was checking out (apparently blubber is fascinating while flooding over linoleum—I wouldn't know) were made
and plans for repeat harassment were suggested. All of this was followed by group back-patting for the original poster; after all, she was
staying strong in the health world and remaining the opposite of Jes
Baker, or the person they preferred to call "It." Those who are willing
to accept that I am a sentient and multifaceted human, made of flesh
and blood, address me by my name. Those who refuse to acknowledge

---

1. One person was facetiously concerned that I confused the name for cookies
as "Genetics," and another was simply embarrassed that I had to buy cookies because I was, after all, a baker and too lazy to do it myself. Regardless, I
learned something new—cookies at the store exist only to be looked at, not
bought. Writing that down for next time.

2. Did you know that all thin people are immortal? Me neither!

my humanity prefer the dehumanizing term that unquestionably categorizes me as nothing more than a detestable object.

Caught off-guard by this detailed experience that I was unaware of in the moment and the emotional violence that followed in the comment section, my internal coping skills were annihilated. I spent the next few days completely unable to function—over self-medicating, spending my days sitting on my couch binge-watching brainless action movies in a state of what felt like incurable numbness. I lacked the ability to do the simplest of tasks like laundry, cooking, or even just brushing my hair for the majority of a week.

Every fiber of my being fights me on sharing these details about my fragility; divulging these moments of emotional powerlessness feels like I am conceding, admitting that the vile persecution techniques used online can indeed devastate their intended target. But the need to be honest about the profound damage these comments can cause, even to me—a person who has honed personal resiliency as both a survival tactic and an empowering life strategy—trumps whatever satisfaction that this confession might bring the megalomaniacs involved.

After recovering from the public vilification, I decided that openly sharing this particular thread with friends would be the next step in aiding my attempt to process the incident. Unsurprisingly, all were shocked by the depth of hate that had found me. They had various reactions: some of uncontrollable rage, some of lost sleep. Some laughed unbelievably at the ludicrousness of it all. There were those who couldn't finish it, and my mother was one of the people so affected by the vitriol that she cried for three days. I was stunned not just by the internet discussion, but also by these visceral reactions. After all, I had been sharing the realities of the harassment I experienced by working online for years, albeit sparingly. And yet I witnessed more anger erupting out of those closest to me than I had ever seen before. Maybe the truth about being a loud, unapologetic fat woman on the internet had finally hit close enough to home for my community to process.

I brought the thread to my therapist, partially so she had an understanding of what I was experiencing and in part to hear her thoughts. As I watched her scroll down through words that made many others physically nauseous, she did little more than raise her eyebrows a couple of times.

I sat silently and waited for her reaction. She finished reading and handed me back the phone. Calmly looking at me, she simply stated: "These people are extraordinarily sick."

It wasn't said in a condemnatory way, nor in a protective way (though I would have appreciated this). It wasn't presented in a reactionary way, but in a way that stated the simple truth.

In a world that praises perceived physical health as the ultimate form of success, these indignant internet-addicted individuals are blue ribbon–award winners in real life. Perhaps strangers walk by them and make silent goals to become "more like that." There is a chance that these people are perpetually inspiring to those who see them out and about. They, after all, have achieved the superficial currency that goes along with a thin and "fit" figure. They are the visual embodiment of wellness culture. Societal accolades are undoubtedly sent their way, congratulating them on their achievement of optimal physical health, yet they are also, ultimately and obviously, some of the most unwell people in existence.

Their obsession to become the physical epitome of health had taken over their lives in a way that had emotionally overrun their soul with emotional sickness. Nancy's simple assessment, in her signature unflappable style, taught me a lesson that I will never forget.

As I reclined on her comfortable red couch, clutching a pillow to my chest while my session came to a close, I started to fully digest this frank truth: you can spend your life becoming the epitome of visual health and still be tragically, shockingly, and profoundly sick.

CHAPTER 11

....

Safety Scares the Shit Out of Me

I'VE BEEN TAUGHT to not talk about my strengths for fear of being labeled a narcissist,[1] but I'm going to ignore that rule right now and tell you something amazing about me: *I'm brave as fuck.*

Brave as in, if I'm asked to do something that terrifies me, I'll usually say yes simply because it terrifies me. Brave as in putting myself in situations that challenge my adaptability skill set because change is difficult for me. Brave as in flying across the world alone because I want to be sure I can be independent. Brave as in quitting my job to work another one that I created and which came with absolutely zero guidance. Brave as in facing mental illness and beating it into submission. Brave as in voicing my opinions in difficult situations. Brave as in standing up to bullies who target me and others, not just online but also in real life. Brave as in speaking the truth when it's unpopular. Brave as in setting high life goals with intentions of keeping all of them. Brave as in accepting that I'm human and still an

....

1. A word we like to abuse whenever we get uncomfortable with a person who possesses a modicum of self-esteem.

okay person when some of those goals don't work out. Brave as in
tackling topics in public places when others wouldn't dare. Brave as
in being comfortable on stage when I know I'll be challenged over
and over again. Brave as in I've fallen down 18,367,209,367,234,897,346
,792,834[2] times and I'm still here standing.

I'm brave as hell in so many ways, yet there is one place in my life
where I have so much fear that it consumes me. It creates barriers
and debilitates me to the point of purposefully sabotaging my life so
I don't have to face this frightening thing . . . ever. My biggest fear?
Honest, committed, transparent, healthy, intimate love.

Scares the absolute shit out of me.

I was told my entire life in multiple ways that I wasn't deserving of such a thing, and for years I bought what they were selling.
I allowed the belief that I wouldn't ever be deserving of real love to
drive my search in partners, and, not surprisingly, I found myself
self-fulfilling those prophecies over and over again. After dozens of
noncommittal dates and several devastating long-term breakups, I
found both feminism (at age *twenty-one*, folks) and body liberation.
I was finally ready to consider rejecting the message of complete
self-hatred.

So, I worked. I worked hard. On being okay on my own. On sitting
with loneliness and my false conviction that I was unworthy. On finding the healing in being alone and valuing myself. Filling my life
with things that were meaningful to me and not compromising my
goals for another's. I dated more confidently, learning the value of
my time. I found power in a way that I needed. Instead of functioning
from a place of scarcity, I balanced decades of passionless, loveless,
sexless, unempowering bullshit with more than a year of passion-
ate, love-filled (for myself and for others), sexy empowerment. I was
single, becoming aware of my value, and free. Everything I wanted,

---

2. A humble approximation.

I could have. When you truly believe that you deserve nothing for most of your life, this is a complete game changer.

What no one told me, though, is that learning to love yourself while being single, barefoot, and fancy-free is the easier part.

Having never extensively invested in someone grounded, balanced, and dedicated to seeing and loving all of me, I had no idea how terrifying it would be. How unnatural it would feel. How I would have to sit on my hands and talk myself out of running away every day.

So, yes, intertwining my life with Andy's was a slow and painfully drawn-out affair.

After spending several nights together playing pool, abusing our favorite bar's jukebox privileges (turns out that the bartender can skip tracks if you play CCR multiple times in a row), and having extraordinary sex until the sun came up, followed by drinking AeroPress coffee while sitting on the back of my car in the morning . . . well, I was ready to drive the six hours to Vegas and stand in front of Elvis in a chapel. He had a better record collection than me, for Chrissakes. Why *wouldn't* we elope immediately after meeting?

This felt fantastical and cinematic to me at the time. In reality, however, my steadfast self-sabotaging routine that had worked so well for me in the past was starting to kick in. I loved to date by starting with a burning fire, then follow up with far too much fun and end with a purposefully controlled burn-out. While I was working on feeling worthy and was making progress, I was still more comfortable getting the high of accepting companionship without actually having to confront the layers buried underneath years of fear by getting truly, emotionally intimate with someone. I would pretend I was ready for something serious, convinced it was the greatest thing ever, then act surprised when I set in motion a purposeful crash and burn. I was more convinced of my worth than ever before. I had taken control of other parts of my life in a way that impressed even me. I wanted love, of course. But that transparent, healthy, balanced intimacy thing? I couldn't look it fully in the eyes. Not yet, anyway.

My energetic approach to everything in life is "LET'S GO DO IT RIGHT NOW!" sometimes knowing I will back out before it gets too real. Andy, not so much. As is constantly true with our relationship even years later, he habitually moves slower than I do. It's almost comical how different we are when it comes to speed.

He wakes up an hour early to acclimate to each new day, leisurely making coffee and lollygagging around the house simply because he can. I, however, set my morning alarm a few minutes later than I should, prizing every extra moment of sleep over the following manic showering, dressing, and dashing out the door. He tells stories with exaggerated pauses, and I recount the day as if I just drank seven Red Bulls. He is a slow and offensive driver; I am a defensive, lane-crossing asshole. He values enjoyment, and I, efficiency. And somehow, the one thing we manage is to get to mutual events on time. I take this as a sign of unparalleled compatibility.

This difference worked in my favor as we dated. I haven't heard many marriage stories that start in Vegas and end well (though my knowledge is limited to the first installment of *The Hangover*), but I do know a drive-through marriage after dating for a month would have been regrettable, no matter our future compatibility. I may not have admitted it at the time, but if he had agreed to my impulsivities in the beginning I would have been freaked out.

So, we may not have driven to Vegas, but I did the emotional equivalent a few weeks later.

After collapsing next to each other for what felt like the millionth time, panting from physical exertion, Saturday night slowly brightened into Sunday morning. Feeling all the endorphins and incapable of creating healthy boundaries, I brazenly suggested that we . . . y'know, kinda, maybe didn't see other people? He inhaled a long breath and turned his face to me before saying, "Well, I think that since I just ended a relationship not too long ago that might not be a great idea right now." If my heart had a face, it would have felt like it had been punched squarely between the eyes.

I instantly reverted to my old coping mechanisms and thoughts. I knew it. Not worthy. Not enough. Too fat. Too needy. Too much. I darted down the hallway so I could cry in the bathroom until I had sufficiently wallowed in enough self-pity to return. After crying myself a pitiful river, I gathered my slightly regulated feelings, scooped up whatever coping mechanisms I could manage, and returned to the bedroom.

With a past checkered with emotionally unavailable partners (self-fulfilling prophesies, remember?), I walked to bed, fully expecting it to be empty, to find Andy in the kitchen making coffee or doing something else that would passively ignore my feelings and the uncomfortable situation. Avoidance and a cold shoulder was what I was used to. I was fully prepared for it, and honestly, I wouldn't have held it against him.

But he was still there, waiting for me under the covers.

Instead of distancing himself and acting as if I hadn't just asked him to date me and then run into the bathroom because of abandonment issues, he was still there. His rumpled hair, sympathetic eyes, and a gentle smile were everything I needed at that moment. Nonjudgmental acceptance that allowed me to crawl under the covers again without feeling like a completely codependent idiot.

He kissed me and said, "I really, really like you. I hope you understand."

"I do." It was an honest statement.

I got it now, 100 percent. He was amazing. He was normal and balanced and capable of making sound decisions. I was also great but came with a tornado of needs, wants, and questions that no one could answer, especially me. I also knew in that moment that I was a person who was going to be challenged by this baffling, balanced male and that matching his pace was going to be good for me.

My reactionary side hated the pace. My responsive side needed the pace. I struggled to balance the two.

I offered an option that we meet in the middle. *Okay, this dude likes me a ton but needs space, and I want to hang out with him 24/7.* I countered with what I thought was a brilliant idea: "How abouuuut instead of being monogamous, we just become each other's #1 Bitch? Y'know . . . as in we're each other's #1 Fuck and Hangout Buddy but can still date other people. The only deal is that if we meet someone else who outranks either one of us, we're transparent and say, 'Sorry, man, but right now you're my #2 Bitch.'"

He laughed. At the absurdity or out of respect for my ingenuity I've never asked, but it was the pact I placed on the table, and, dare I say, it was a really good one. That night started our (now) unbreakable bond of honesty. The foundation was set from the beginning. I made laurel-leaf-decorated mugs with #1 Bitch prominently featured on the front to seal the noncommittal deal.

I have always been pretty extra.

I tried to do my part and follow through with the whole "Let's date other people thing," finding myself on other dates at The Shelter—a dingy bar full of Reagan portraits and lighting from the fifties—*Mhmming* and *Ahhhing,* trying to feign interest over their boring-as-hell explanations of PhD programs, which were apparently the most fascinating opportunities on the planet. Maybe they were. I have no idea and couldn't have given less of a fuck. My mind had little bandwidth for anyone except for my bearded jazz dude with great shoes. Each date ended with their "I'd love to see you again" and my noncommittal "Yeah, maybe!" Other times, I would meet with nice people for a drink, attempting to find commonality but eventually excusing myself so I could walk across the street to an art gallery opening where Andy's charcoal Frank Zappa portrait was featured.

I tried. I may have sucked at it, but no one can say that I didn't try.

Eventually, the inevitable happened, and we became permanent #1 Bitches.

Six months after our Monogamous Bitch commitment, though, I started showing up to therapy in a full-blown panic. "This guy is too balanced, Nancy. It's weird and totally unnatural." I tried to breathe normally to ease the anxiety that was causing me to collapse on her couch, while my body pulsed with a THIS MAY BE DEADLY fight-or-flight response. "He doesn't rampage or try to manipulate situations. He doesn't try to hurt my feelings to get his way or walk out when things are hard. I don't know what the fuck to do with him, honestly."

The beginning, as it turned out, had been easy. The long, drawn-out dating experience that had tested my sense of worth was easier than this. I had stumbled upon honest, unwavering, committed, transparent, healthy, intimate love, and I didn't know what the fuck to do with it.

But, I was committed to investing everything I had in this bizarrely wonderful relationship. There was something special about this man, and I loved him. I really, really loved him.

....

Unsolicited and potentially disastrous relationship advice: When you have "some emotional investment but not too much" with your new supercrush that you hang out with all the time, make it a point to play "I've Never: The Game of Truth," the early-2000s board game designated as "The Best Drinking Game Ever!" by Anonymous and featured in *Newsweek* and *Playboy*.

Imagine a board game that looks a little like Candy Land, but instead of landing in the Candy Cane Forest, you land on a square that requires you to pick up a card that asks, "What is the most bizarre place you've ever had sex?"

The box design is outdated, purple, orange, and just as hideous as everything else from that decade,[3] which only adds to its charm.

Play it multiple times with your crush until you run out of cards or questions. Play it until you've ripped off all of your old relationship bandages. Play it until you're no longer afraid to ask any question. Play it until you drunkenly work through sordid details to the point where they no longer hold any power. Play it until they want to hide the card deck.

Then, maybe, don't play it anymore.

Don't play this with your parents.

Do play it with your best friends.

We played it, just as I was starting to accept that maybe I could have this balanced, honest, vulnerable partnership thing I've always wanted. That timing worked out as well, because now I find myself in an exceptional relationship where we don't lie.

I look at that sentence and think how impossible it sounds. Considering that, in general, I think most human beings are inherent liars, the overall likelihood of this happening feels minuscule. And it probably is. But I have somehow found myself in several relationships where complete honesty is the norm—with my mother, with two friends, and with my partner.

I can't explain how important that last one is.

We have not lied to each other once. We did bend the truth a couple of times in the beginning—once when he told me I nailed "9 to 5" at karaoke (not my range, and I know it) and once when I said I would be happy to sleep on the couch (I hated the couch but hated his tiny twin bed—which would comfortably fit an infant but certainly not two adults—even more)—but even then, we called them out and replaced them with truthful clarity. From the beginning, we built an understanding that even if it was difficult, the truth was and

....
3. Except for Nsync's J.C. He was a total babe.

always would be the most important thing. It started when we had nothing to really lose—his "No" to dating exclusively and our pact to be honest about being #1 Bitches. It continued through every card of "I've Never," and through every time a part of me craved drama or uncertainty. We started from the beginning, though I didn't know at the time how critical building that foundation would be. And after coming from dysfunctional, secretive relationships, I still can't believe that this is possible.

There have been some hard truths that we've had to bravely say. Things that no one really wants to hear. But we had them; all of the discussions that we feared most. Tears, definitely. Anger, occasionally. But always a resolution that only comes out of honest processing done together. I've never met a mechanically minded person with such incredible communication skills.

We've been conditioned by God knows who at this point that sometimes we have to lie to our person in order to spare their feelings; that this is a service we're doing because we "love them." There is another option: being completely honest in the most compassionate way possible. It all comes down to using love as a bridge between safety and truth.

Somehow, we've navigated multiple deaths, unemployment, job changes, self-sabotage, planning a conference I was incapable of planning, pending lawsuits, getting a dog (surprisingly difficult), family integration, mental breakdowns, road trips gone wrong, and that awful summer with one of the worst bedbug infestations our exterminator had ever seen. That last one was rough, and my skin still crawls when writing about it. But truth and kindness create safety, and damn if we didn't need that fucking safety throughout the time we've been together.

Not only is this trust part of our daily feeling of safety, but it's also become an integral part of my healing when it comes to my body.

CHAPTER 12

Three Vaginas

IT WAS 9:00 P.M., which meant it was time to crawl into bed; I had adopted Andy's Old Person Bedtime Routine ever since we had moved in together two years previously and it became convenient for everyone. That, and I realized that I'm a much nicer person when I get an appropriate amount of sleep.

The house we had found together was my personal dream house; perhaps in comparison to others my dream house bar might seem pretty low, but let's just say that it means I'm easy to please. It had high ceilings, wood floors that complained after having been walked on for hundreds of years, giant windows covered in hard-water stains, and a worn clawfoot bathtub. I added a vintage couch in the living room and a steel baking table in the kitchen and, after standing back to admire my work, I gave a mental shoutout to hipster me for thinking her worth was defined by owning awesome things. Though *I* no longer believed that, because *she* had I was left with an appreciation of great vintage interior taste.

The only thing missing from our home that would have made it truly perfect was a black-and-white tiled floor in the bathroom, which is currently painted a dark brown. I am too lazy to cover it with linoleum so I instead hung several five-dollar full-length mirrors to open up the space. Andy lay in bed at 9:01 p.m. (he really is sleep's biggest fan) but, not ready to join him, I stood sideways in front of one of the mirrors, analyzing my stomach, whose shape had changed dramatically over the last couple of years.

I used to have a method for evaluating my stomach and then determining my worth as a person. It first started in my early twenties. The equation was simple: if I could suck it in and not tell that it existed, I was just fine. After continuing to gain weight,[1] the new counter-equation became the following: as long as my profile showed that my boobs were bigger than my stomach, I was okay. When this was no longer an option, I conceded that at least if I could suck it in and it *then* protruded less than my boobs, I would allow myself to go out into public with my head held high . . . ish.

I've been an asshole to myself for a really long time.

The low light in the bathroom and the dark floors frustrated me, but nowhere near as much as my body did that night. Its rapid expansion over the last couple years still felt both unfamiliar and shameful, something that people tease about when you "relax" and "let yourself go" while in a comfortable relationship. Maybe our relationship played a part. But I am convinced that it has a lot more to do with the complete lifestyle change that had happened since we'd started making out in a shared home. Our jobs had changed within the same time period, both of us leaving behind more physically active jobs for work that was beneficial in every way but required less action and way more computer work. We ate differently as our grocery shopping combined. We went out less, as we preferred the comfort of our home, each other's company and copious amounts of cheap wine over almost anything else. I had also at that point given

....
1. My current vodka tonic and Capri diet *clearly* failed me.

up dieting completely; the more I learned about how much energy I was spending on institutionalized starvation the more averse to it I became. I no longer restricted my eating, and my body responded to all of these things by creating a silhouette I was unfamiliar with. I had been writing about body image for years and had learned to embrace the body I had years ago. But the figure I saw in front of me that night felt new, too new, and I was horrified.

There was no sucking in of my stomach at this point. My chest was no competition anymore, my belly folding over and resting on top of the rest of my body. I now call it my cute fanny pack; that night, I called it failure. I had to come to terms with the fact that I was now physically wider while standing sideways than when I faced front.

My eyes roamed over my thighs, which had gathered extra skin that pouched on each leg, creating V-shaped creases where a smooth surface had been before. Self-hatred started to accumulate so rapidly that I simply couldn't handle staring at myself a second longer. There it was, even after years of honesty and vulnerability: I was unworthy, again. My body was still too much. I looked in the mirror and decided that Andy deserved a confession. Knowing was better than not knowing, and he needed to realize what he was dealing with before he spent another moment with this beastly body.

I owed him a come-to-Jesus talk, and he needed it *now*.

I burst into the bedroom. Andy was cocooned in his blanket and turned to face the noise of our bedroom door banging open hard enough that it hit the wall. I climbed up on the bed and stood next to him.

"WAKE UP AND LOOK AT THIS," I demanded, much louder than necessary or intended, my naked body towering over his sleepy head. "LOOK AT MY THREE VAGINAS."

I was beyond caring about how deranged I appeared. Everything was secondary to the fact that he needed to see me for what I was: a hideous, blubbery mammoth that he had been tricked into committing to for the rest of his life.

"I HAVE THREE VAGINAS, AND YOU NEED TO KNOW THIS," I bellowed, repeating the fact in case he had missed it the first time. I grabbed my overlapping stomach, counting aloud—"ONE," I pointed to my thigh's folding skin and then pulled it for dramatic effect. "TWO." I then pointed to my actual genitalia, "THREE" I roared. "I HAVE THREE VAGINAS, AND I DON'T KNOW HOW IT HAPPENED, BUT YOU NEED TO LOOK AT THEM SO YOU KNOW WHAT YOU'RE DATING."

Narrator: Jes had finally lost her fucking mind.

I'm still unsure how he didn't howl with laughter at this bizarre and unexpected performance, but I'm sure that, sensing my exasperation, he didn't dare. G'bless him. It was the right choice, and he knew it.

He lay there for a moment in the quiet, taking in my entire naked body towering over him, my hands digging into my hips, face full of rage.

"Babe," he said benevolently, a small corner of his mouth twitching as he tried to maintain a straight face. "I'm going to tell you something."

"WHAT?" I was resolute. I was hideous, and there was nothing he could say to convince me otherwise. *Don't you dare underestimate me, Andy,* I thought. *You know I'm smarter than that.*

He paused and looked me directly in my eyes. "Babe, you only have one vagina."

A moment of silence.

God damn him and his common sense. How in the world was I supposed to refute a biological fact? It was a dirty, dirty trick.

"You only have one vagina, and it's wonderful, and the rest of your body is too. You're sexy all the way around, and I love every part of you."

I stood in silence, trying my best to remain skeptical. Andy and I had promised each other complete honesty and had successfully kept this commitment for years. I begrudgingly realized that this inevitably applied to his feelings about my body as well. He was telling the truth, whether I could accept it or not.

"Do you want to cuddle?" he offered. My resolution started to crumble, and my arms fell to my sides.

My argument was significantly perforated by his annoyingly simple common sense and the fact that we had made that important pact to always be honest with each other, regardless of its potentially terrifying ramifications. I had just shown him the truth of my insecurities, and he had responded with genuine adoration anyway. I resigned myself to a night of confrontational failure. As I lay down next to him, he pulled his blanket out from underneath him, covered me, and pulled me close.

Narrator: Defeated by logic, she was forced to acknowledge that someone loved her just the way she was.

"Never forget that you're the love of my life, okay?" he said as he kissed my forehead. I nodded and continued to hug him while he put in earplugs, because no matter how sexy I may be, I snore like a motherfucker.

....

Steeping our beginnings in authenticity has created a space for trust like I've never experienced before. This and only this has allowed me to believe him when he tells me how perfect my body is. How it's just as sexy as it was when I met him forty pounds ago.

His body has changed too. It's become softer. More comfortable. Less of a visual performance and more of the human that I love. Watching his body change as well and finding it just as sexy as before has added to the proof I needed that maybe it is possible for him to do the same.

The only conclusion I can draw from this is that for us, love and sexiness are inseparable.

That's hard for me to process, perhaps because I've believed for most of my life that I could never have one or be the other. But here they are, intertwined and restructuring the way I see my world. I've learned from experience that while we don't talk much about it, sexiness is not purely visual. It also stems from untouchable love and being able to see someone in their wholeness. In this way, my stomach is "part of the package."

Most days, accepting all of this is a painfully slow process. But there is forced progress; my internal beliefs are often challenged by what he says to me on a daily basis.

When he passes me in the kitchen and says, "Mmmm, Babe, I love that ass," I don't hear "I love that ass"; instead, I hear "I'm complimenting your ass so you can't tell that I'm ignoring your repulsive stomach." I'm a master at warping even the sincerest body compliments.

My old coping strategy of hiding, crying, and internalizing self-created toxic shit was exhausting, but it always felt safer than asking for what I really wanted. The lock on my old bathroom was the handiest way to bar my partner from communicating with me while I loudly sobbed. That shit never worked, by the way. Not in the long run.

But now, it's different. There is room between us to ask the scariest things. There is safety in voicing what I've never been able to voice before. Now, I just ask what I need to know, no matter how much my insides are twisting.

"But Babe . . . do you also love my stomach?" Giving my biggest fears a voice is nerve-racking, even with infinite trust. Because I know he'll be honest . . . even if it's hard to hear.

"I do." He always hugs me after my vulnerable questioning, his hand lowering and caressing my stomach, where it feels the scariest. It's a sensation I am still unable to fully process—a loving touch on my most offending body part. But I'm not done. "But, do you like, tolerate my stomach because it's part of me and inevitably attached to the rest of me? . . . I get it, if that's the case. I would if I were you." This, I am confident in. My stomach is the last frontier of body parts I have failed to accept.

His brown eyes are remarkably kind. "Babe, I love your belly. It's sexy, and you are beautiful."

I used to feel guilty about needing partner validation, until I realized that I've always allowed my friends and family to assist in countering my bullshit beliefs around body image, to help me relearn. And yet, I wasn't allowing my partner into that circle. I finally decided that he just might be a helpful person to assist in my healing.

Part of all this healing was understanding that how he feels about my body aligns with how he feels about my heart, about the rest of me. This, in addition to intimately knowing a super fat babe myself. I was completely unable to deny her physical sexiness, and this broke my heart open in a million wonderful ways. Even after years of deprogramming my brain around size bias, I was still judging my own fat body in a detrimental and suffocating way. Being unable to ignore the mirroring of my body in hers reminded me that *damn* fat bodies are sexy. Hella sexy. And with this truth comes the reminder that this includes my body as well.

These moments are still necessary for me because I'm just not "there" yet when it comes to total body acceptance. Some days, sure. But not all the time. Sometimes, I need someone else to see the sexiness. I can't help but wonder if we all need that kind of help at some point. I know *for a fact* that all bodies are inherently beautiful. My years of body-image work have taught me this undeniable truth. But often when it comes to ourselves, this belief falters. Often the one who struggles to see the beauty in us . . . is us.

There is still a part of me that worries about becoming "too much" in the long term. That he will eventually become exhausted from needing to address my insecurities. But every time that thought crosses my mind, he reminds me about the maggots.

The first time I asked if it was too much to continually reassure me that my body was okay, he sat me down and explained why he would never tire of this by sharing his favorite *Ghostbuster*'s episode.

He broke my paradigm with a goddamn *Ghostbuster*'s episode from the nineties.

The episode he shared went something like this: The Ghostbusters were struggling with a villainous apparition that takes the shape of whatever that person was most afraid of. In true "must stretch this into a full thirty-minute show" fashion, each person tries to eradicate the ghost, each failing spectacularly, until someone realizes, "HEY! I'm not scared of what you're scared of! We should team up and fight each other's worst fears instead of confronting our own while alone!" They did just that, each terrifying apparition tackled by a person un-affected until they, of course, won. Hallelujah, run the credits.

"One of the scary things was maggots," Andy said. "And you know what? Your maggots are not my maggots. I'll crush your maggots for you, and you can crush my maggots for me."

My maggots take the form of insurmountable moments of body shame, and he is determined to crush those fuckers every time. While I work to fight off body hatred, not even aiming for body love, but simply a consistent acceptance of neutrality, he does the work of loving my body for me. He carries the torch effortlessly. Patiently. Lovingly. It's not hard for him.

Our trust helps it resonate just a little bit deeper each time. I've got a long way to go, but I've also got an adorable, bearded Ghost-buster on my side.

....

I used to secretly wonder if the fact that Andy and I were no lon-ger banging seventeen times a day meant we were broken. And unfortunately sometimes I find comments from bitter men underneath articles that I've written that attempt to confirm those fears. After publishing a (difficult to write but damn-well needed) piece called "I've Gained Weight. So What?" in which I unapologetically addressed the fact that my body had changed and the world had *not* ended, this gem appeared below it:

> "Your husband might be verbally supportive, but pay attention to his biological attraction limits. Keep in mind there is no such thing as erectile dysfunction, only wife-let-herself-go dysfunction. Once that happens, a man is pretty much done having sex and stops 'trying' in general. And no, you'll never fully recover from that, even if the weight comes back off."

It was posted on a third party's website, so I didn't have my go-to option of deleting and blocking. Instead, I sat with this stranger's assessment of my life, body, sex life, and relationship for a few moments.

After the normal mental process I go through when I have the blessing of reading these sorts of comments (that often goes something like: *Fuck you,* then *Wow, somebody got burned in real life,* and then *Whatever, dude*), I found myself coming back to it.

It still bothered me, and I hated that it still bothered me.

I tried to parse out why. This keyboard addict (we'll call him Todd[2]) was purposefully playing on a fat woman's greatest fear: that no matter how much your partner loved you, if you gained any amount of weight they would inevitably slam the front door on your

....

2. Lindy West calls all "anonymous internet dill-holes" the same name: Kevin. I personally claim Todd. Why? Because according to a random online pie chart they are the only ones who still wear cargo shorts, something that is now apparently irrelevant, much like the opinions of the people who comment on my relationship and body. I HEREBY CHRISTEN ALL OF THESE INTERLOPERS "TODD."

hideous physique with a "I NEVER SIGNED UP FOR THIS SHIT!" and never look back.

He not only left this as evidence to come back and point to so future generations would see that "he called it" after Andy made his inevitable escape from his fat partner but also so other women who read this article would absorb that a "man" (aka the person who is sanctioned by society to decide the attractiveness of all women) would surely make their worst fears come true.

Through his commentary, Todd was trying to take away not only whatever trust I had in myself as a fat woman, but also my trust in my partner and the radical truthfulness that our relationship was founded on.

Damn, these people need better hobbies.

What Todd didn't know while posting this purposefully agitating "truth bomb" is that I have been in that exact situation before. *Several times, actually.*

It started with a carny.[3] My first long-term relationship with a person who I met while sitting on the curb in front of Tucson's only punk bar. A person I instantly fell for.

How could I not? He was lanky, 6′7″, and looked unbelievable in tight black jeans and a disintegrating hoodie that was patched with dental floss. This, in addition to the fact that he was covered in tattoos, had four-inch stretched ears, cursed like a sailor (appropriate for his future job on a ship), and was twenty years older than me (several decades of sexual experience that I didn't have as a rebellious ex-Mormon was a plus), and he actually worked for the goddamn circus.

He was also emotionally unavailable, untrusting enough to sleep with a baseball bat, recovering from a lifetime of hard drugs, and had

....
3. You heard me correctly—a goddamn carny. More specifically, a lead rigger (aka the suspension professional whose job it is to ensure that the acrobats don't die) for the Ringling Bros. and Barnum & Bailey Circus.

a deep addiction to alcohol. At the knowledgeable age of twenty-one, I was positive that this rough-around-the-edges, mosh-pit-loving, completely dysfunctional sex addict was my soul mate.[4]

And so, I fell in love with the Christian Grey of carnies.

After a year of dating semi–long distance (note to self: never again), I applied for as many credit cards as the banks would give me, maxed them out on a plane ticket and four enormous bags of the sexiest underwear I could find, and headed to Denver. I was ready to live with the circus while it was stationed in Colorado.

It was apparent upon my arrival that when it comes to the circus there is no splendor, color, or flair. Whatever was presented during their performance was perfectly countered by real life behind the scenes. Each car ran amok with perversion, grime, vulgarity, and renegades running from whatever life they had come from.

I loved every part of it.

I spent my time while Derek was at work with his brooding next-door neighbor, Victor. Russian, in his late fifties, and visibly weathered by years of emotional pain, Victor usually worked as a chef in the galley but had been asked to take a "temporary break from work" after showing up intoxicated five days in a row. This meant that we both had plenty of time to adapt to his habit of drinking vodka straight from the bottle for breakfast, and we became fast friends, passing the hours listening to music, him lamenting the fact that his ex-wife had swindled him out of his restaurant and me preparing meals for the night with his supervision. Evenings were spent with Derek in tattoo parlors, playing board games with other stagehands, and huddled around the fire pit sharing inappropriate stories.

The ugly felt insightful, the traumatic was electrifying, the grime was beguiling, and painting the town red always seemed like the

....
4. It's now very apparent that I spent my early twenties doing my best to prove to everyone that my frontal lobe was nowhere near developed. I did a *damn* good job, if I do say so myself.

proper thing to do. It was twisted and magical; it was perfect until it wasn't.

Ever the irresponsible twenty-two-year-old, I missed my plane and drove back to the train to spend the time before my next flight with the man I loved. I found Derek fast asleep with *Scarface* playing in the background. Breaking the most basic cardinal relationship rule, I took this opportunity to look at his text messages.

Maybe it saved me future pain. Maybe it didn't. It's irrelevant to guess at this point. All I know is that while scrolling, wide-eyed, through the graphic sexting to and from an ex, I felt my fear of inadequacy solidify. These texts proved what I had been taught my entire life. I wasn't sexy enough. I wasn't satisfying enough. I simply wasn't enough.

This, followed by the dramatic exit of my second partner, who made it clear that he didn't want anything to do with my body after it started gaining weight, was exactly what Mr. Todd had predicted. I even experienced it again while casually dating someone for a few months and then never hearing from him again after meeting his friend, who obviously didn't approve of my body, at Hooters.[5] But what Todd didn't realize is that he wasn't telling me anything new; I was all too familiar with the fallout that he had described in detail. I knew exactly what it looked and felt like. I'd been there. Multiple times.

I knew the signs better than most, and this wasn't something I ever forgot, not even when beginning the stunningly safe relationship I have now.

For the first few years with Andy, I worried that the same thing would happen between the two of us, anticipating a similar ending to this relationship as I had experienced with my other failed relationships. I was hypervigilant in looking for the signs that would

....
5. This is what they call a *red flag*, Jes.

eventually lead to my deserved abandonment. But what I failed to take into account was the fact that I was no longer the person who had experienced those dramatic relationship endings. I had since developed a sense of self, an adequate amount of self-esteem, sophisticated communication skills, and, perhaps most important, well-founded knowledge of what *didn't work* when it came to a partnership. In the words of the water-damaged tear-off calendar that rests on my friend's bathroom sink: "I know that old, negative patterns no longer limit me and I let them go with ease."

All of this led me into an authentic and transparent relationship with Andy who believes in honesty and commitment. Oh, *and* he is fully aware that bodies change over time. Bonus.

A list of things that have impacted our sex life:

1. Getting an eight-week-old puppy that doesn't sleep at night (or ever)[6]

2. My inevitable depression flare-ups

3. Complete and utter exhaustion

4. Dry shampoo[7]

5. Having his family staying in the next room over (just kidding; that doesn't stop us)

6. The internalization of the fucked-up notion that if your body changes your relationship is doomed

....

6. But he also gets so excited to see me that he pees himself. It's absolutely disgusting but also oddly endearing, so I guess we'll keep him.

7. This marvelous invention has made it easy to convince the public that I shower regularly. Unfortunately, this doesn't translate into the bedroom, where Andy is impressively skilled at discerning that it has been at *least* three days since I used body wash and hot water.

7. Allowing other people's experiences to convince me that my body isn't sexy or deserving of my partner's attention (*get out of my bedroom, strangers!*)

8. Writing this hella draining and traumatizing memoir

9. Attempting to talk dirty while mimicking Alison Brie's faux Russian accent from the TV show *Glow*[8]

10. Feeling like a total piece of shit for whatever reason (shockingly, this isn't a huge turn-on)

11. Being in different countries and not having cell reception or Wi-Fi

12. Beauty and diet culture reminding us daily that sex is only for people in perfume ads

Things that haven't ever impacted our sex life:

1. My body

2. My body physically changing

3. His body

4. His body physically changing

5. Our bodies

6. Our bodies physically changing together

7. High-waisted underwear

I've been forced to realize that our bodies, no matter what they look like, have never been and never will be the problem. I pride myself on being a critical thinker and introspection enthusiast, and yet I'm always taken aback at how so many simple truths escape me.

---

8. It's equal parts hilarious and humiliating. I do NOT recommend.

Finally, I've started to let them sink in. After years with Andy, I surmised, *Well, maybe it's time to give myself permission to just be . . . myself.* I'm not entirely certain, but when I first thought it kind of felt like the beauty industry shed a small tear and shriveled a little on the inside.

It's unfortunate that I allowed other people and ideas inside our bedroom, giving them permission to reinforce negative body-image cycles, which easily perpetuate themselves. Nothing makes me feel sexier than sex, and nothing makes me disconnect from my body more than refusing sex because I've decided I'm unworthy. The disconnection often causes me to spiral, leading to less connection between me, my body, and my partner until the situation feels like it's almost too difficult to reconcile. Fortunately, it's never become irreparable. These cycles ultimately boil down to my need for mental reconditioning, something I've been working on for what feels like forever. But I am positive that I'm capable of rejecting the idea that I am unlovable, not sexy, not allowed to change, forever undesirable, or any other negative messaging I've been sold.[9] It's not a simple task, but I'm already seeing progress.

Love is about more than just bodies. To realize this now feels embarrassing, but also more beautiful than I can describe.

I don't say this with any air of superiority. I don't share this so you can compare your relationship to mine.[10] I say this because the world will try to convince you that not only can you not trust yourself in feeling adequate and worthy, but you also can't trust your partner.[11] Don't listen.

....

9. I refuse to let capitalism dictate my sex life, damnit.

10. Please don't do this. Ever.

11. How can I be sure that we are completely honest with each other? I suppose I can't predict the future, but right now I trust myself when assessing our relationship. And I sure as hell trust myself more than I trust any other person—especially keyboard warriors named Todd.

Our bodies can be an important part of our relationship, something we love to get hot and bothered about. Sex, intercourse, screwing around, copulation, coitus, monkey business, naughty nooky, lovemaking, fucking, getting it on, fab fornication, banging out, hanky-panky, physical intimacy . . . feel free to describe physical connection any way you like. I'm a fan of them all. That body-to-body connection is an important aspect of many relationships; it certainly is in our case. But it's important to remember that our bodies are also only a segment of what makes up "us," our partnership consisting of so many more pieces than just our physical desires. Sometimes, our bodies serve the simplest purpose: allowing us to lie next to each other, my head on his shoulder, listening to audiobooks in the dark while he sleepily kisses my forehead. It's then that my body does not need to be anything other than a vessel through which he can love all of me at the same time . . . and it is in those simplest of moments when everything feels okay.

CHAPTER 13

....

So, Have You Ever
Thought About Dieting?

I MAKE a point of publicly sharing online when I have a "bad body day" so that I don't contribute to the myth that says, "You can reach the point where you never doubt or hate yourself!" I continue to do it, even though the comment section, while often filled with appreciative thank yoooooooous (I love excessive o's), becomes a dumping ground for unsolicited proposals on foolproof ways to fix my apparently alarming lack of self-esteem.

I find myself wishing desperately that someone would give me a cat (fuck dollars, I just want cats) every time some ignoramus (or seven) suggests their unique and "revolutionary" idea: *Well, have you ever thought about dieting?*

I would have three hundred cats. I would be the overjoyed owner of a cat chateau—all made possible by impertinent and uninspired internet comments. That's what I really want in life. That and a vintage clawfoot tub that doubles as a hot tub. Do these exist? If not, someone needs to get on that.

On a certain level, I get it. I've spent most of my life believing that dieting was the ingenious solution to all body-image issues. And there's a good reason for this: we are all so resistant to ditch this seemingly simple solution because diet culture has reinforced that restriction is a form of self-control, starvation is a spiritual practice, and if we can reach utopic obedience in these ways we will have instant access to heaven, where self-esteem, validation, and worthiness are liberally doled out with fistfuls of glitter and endless praise. All you have to do is become a physical replica of Megan Fox, Scarlett Johansson, or Kendall Jenner, and they'll let you walk through those cloud-enshrouded gates. No biggie.

There is so much perfunctory feel-good bullshit that seems to go along with our participation in dieting. Whether you're in the midst of the newest trend in food restriction or contemplating which diet book speaks to your soul, you will inevitably be met with back pats and copious amounts of encouragement. Make no mistake: all that praise is a purposeful tactic to keep you coming back.

And if you were to actually lose weight (however temporary it may be), you can plan on having a socially constructed red carpet woven out of congratulatory remarks rolled out in front of you by nearly every person you know. With weight loss comes the acknowledgment that you are an awe-inspiring role model worthy of admiration and worship.

Diets have become the dazzling and fictional expressway to becoming thin, something that we've all been taught is one of the most important things we can be.

When asked online if I have ever tried dieting, I often let the other readers handle the question. In real life, time constraints usually don't allow a full explanation for this type of internet fuckery, so I just laugh, leave it to brilliant followers, and walk away. Here, however, I have the luxury of presenting a list that just might enlighten those with that same burning question or those who come back with "Well, how many have you tried?"

The Ice Cream Diet (Age Twelve)

By eighth grade, I was fully aware that my body was a moral failure. This obviously affected my middle-school popularity (JK, there was none) and put my weight in the forefront of my mind. Not to worry, though; even at that young age I had a moment of brilliance.

One afternoon during lunch period, in between turns at playing Bullshit (which I called Bologna because I was one of those insufferable Holy Rollers who silently prays for sinners to make it to heaven[1]), I glanced at the nutrition labels on all of the food that sat on my tray. I calculated the total, from those numbers guesstimated the calories of the unmarked food, and, with every ounce of twelve-year-old genius I possessed, realized that the amount of calories in an ice cream Drumstick was significantly less than those in the meal in front of me.

Holy shit.

I had finally figured out how to lose weight.

I was equipped with enough diet knowledge from my father at that point to understand that if you put a tiny bit of calories into your body instead of a bunch of them you could probably trick your body into losing weight.[2] Armed with this simple math, I quickly constructed the "How could this possibly go wrong?" Drumstick Diet.

Before you call me out for concocting this ridiculous weight-loss scheme, know that there are grown-ass adults out there who have

---

1. How did I even have friends?

2. P.S. "Calories in, calories out" is an insulting oversimplification and when used across the board is unreliable AF, but I was twelve, so cut me some slack.

written and published a book about how "The Peanut Butter Diet" will help you lose ten pounds in three days or something. So, keep that judgment to yourself.

Every lunch period, instead of spending my money on a tray of milk, pizza, an apple, and an unidentifiable side, I would march to the counter and order my ice cream cone. I would then self-righteously stride back to my friends and join in on the ongoing game of Bologna.

I usually lost the game because I suck at both lying and cards, but I didn't give a fuck. I had ice cream and was going to lose weight. Winning a card game didn't matter.

This went on for months, and I walked back to the table each day, chest puffed up with pride. I was doing my civic duty. I was following all the rules. I was dieting, fixing my body, *and* eating delicious food. Why hadn't the adults figured out this yet? The Ice Cream Cone Diet made me feel like a goddamn hero.

I managed to keep this information to myself for quite a while, but one day on the way home from school I found myself sharing my brilliant weight-loss plan with my grandma.

The next day, I was confronted by my mother, who was horrified that my diet consisted of vanilla ice cream, peanuts, and chocolate-flavored plastic. She demanded that I return to the regularly scheduled cafeteria lunch. If I was a true rebel, I would have explained that the amount of calcium and protein found in my new and improved lunch plan was more than enough nutrition for a growing preteen, but instead I—being the exceptionally obedient child I was raised to be—frowned and promised to never do it again.

Thanks for nothing, Grandma.

The Weigh Down Workshop Diet (Age Thirteen)

For twelve weeks my aunt, mother, and I attended a religious-based weight-loss program called "Weigh Down Workshop." It was held in a generic Christian church classroom with tiny school chairs that were *definitely* not made for fat people (perhaps the discomfort could inspire even more weight loss?). We brought three things with us:

1. Our workbook, "Exodus Out of Egypt"

2. Sheer desperation to become smaller

3. Faith that God could make it happen

Week after week, the group leader would haul out the rolling metal cart that held an enormously thick television (still in the nineties, mind you) and pop in that week's inspirational VHS tape. Each one featured the same thin, blonde woman with enormous hair named Gwen Shamblin. She spoke the holy truth with her hypnotic Southern accent, preaching about pious portion control all while wearing an ear mic—it was impressive technology, considering the decade. Hands-free microphones and Jesus as your diet companion? It was clear to all of us that this was some *legit shit.*

We spent our group time watching recorded lectures interspersed with tacky theatrical skits about leaving half of a hamburger at that restaurant and filling our longing hearts not with food but with the love of God. Takeaway: if you couldn't drop those pounds, it's not because it wasn't possible. It was because you needed to become better friends with Jesus.

Considering that I participated in this program eighteen years ago, I thought I would do a quick Google search to see what Gwen was up to.

Top Google prediction results:

1. Weigh Down Workshop Cult

2. Where is Gwen Shamblin now?

3. Weigh Down Workshop reviews

Considering that Weigh Down Workshop critics are often compared to Satan by its devout followers, #1 speaks for itself. Number 3 was answered the first search result as well.

After searching for answers for the second question, I discovered that Gwen is still working hard at the "pray your weight away" program, just with hair that is now twice as tall as her actual face. Someone give that woman an award.

While it seemed to help my aunt for a short amount of time, the only thing I remember taking away from the program was that if there was a food that was your kryptonite you should eat it until you hate it and voilà! Problem solved.[3] And if that didn't work? Pray harder.

I can't remember if my thirteen-year-old body lost weight after turning it over to God. I repeated the program several times, which could mean that it either worked extremely well or not at all.

Only God knows.

The Body for Life Diet (Age Fifteen)

The *Body for Life* book was a staple that sat on top of the back of our family's toilet for years, offering moral inspiration while you took care of business.

On the inside of each cover were dozens of before-and-after pictures: the before images of men and women were photographed in dim light with their protruding stomachs and muffin tops[4] prominently featured. Next to each of these was their after picture—a professional studio photo in which each was wearing a bikini or

---

3. Thrilled with this option, I, with permission from God himself, ate chocolate pudding until I was physically ill. Given the fact that I still love chocolate pudding, it seems as though this might not be the most effective advice.

4. Inarguably the best part of a muffin, for the record.

revealing shorts with an unnatural amount of body oil slathered over their rock-hard abs and bulging muscles.

What teenager could argue with such obviously amazing results?

The founder—the hunky Bill Phillips—graced the cover in a tight black shirt with short sleeves that showed off not only his impressively muscular arms but also the dream body underneath the fabric as well. His smirk promised the same results . . . if you dared to join in.

My parents and I worshiped three books in this order: the Book of Mormon, the Bible, and *Body for Life*.

Inspired by the "obviously attainable" results, we all implemented the strict diet (a shit ton of cottage cheese and broccoli) as well as the workouts, which were meant to build one on top of the other until yes, you TOO could become a greasy body builder. So, I joined my parents at the gym, and Phillips became our second prophet.

My mom uses his cookbook to this day.

The SlimFast Diet (Age Sixteen)

Finally equipped with a car, a job, and marginal freedom, I spent the majority of my income on Avon cosmetics and cases of SlimFast from Walmart. Feeling hungry? Drink a SlimFast. Feeling fat? Drink a SlimFast. Feeling anything at all? Drink a SlimFast.

Milk Chocolate (can we just call it Milk Chalk-late already?) was my preferred flavor and became the substitute for most of my meals. My ego soared every time I chose a can of lukewarm brown sludge over substantial food.

The Diet Pills and Cross-Country Diet (Age Seventeen)

Unable to purchase diet pills for myself and more determined than ever to become the epitome of American beauty, I pleaded with my mom to buy them for me until she caved. I sat in the car as she ran into GNC and returned with what I was sure was going to be the answer to *all* of my problems, which nothing else had been able to fix yet. Science and chemicals in the form of pills would be the answer this time. I was sure of it.

Ingesting these every day while hating every moment spent running cross-country was bound to do the trick. I had no doubts.

But I was seventeen and was occasionally known to be wrong. My heart, breaking more and more each day, saw zero "improvement."

Because they cost the same as five haircuts (and I was teenager-style broke), I once again begged my mom to do the dirty work for me and request a refund. She begrudgingly returned to GNC, did as I asked, and was apparently looked up and down before being questioned by the clerk as to whether she had actually dieted AND exercised while taking them.

She returned to the car, humiliated. We sat in silence for a few minutes, sharing in the shame that impacted us both. We drove away while she vehemently vowed to never purchase something like that for me again. I couldn't blame her.

The Rice Diet (Age Eighteen)

Mormon colleges, as previously mentioned, are not about gaining an education. They are designed for getting married.

This goal was to be achieved through regular visits to the campus gym while listening to Sean Hannity. The gym lifestyle didn't appeal to my new roommate, Brittany, an angsty and unapproachable freshman who wore only black and was never seen without her headphones, noisily beating every surface with wooden drumsticks—which she couldn't even hear over her music, but god, *we* did. I avoided her for the most part, ignoring both her and her habits . . . until she started eating nothing but white rice.

Every day. Breakfast, lunch, and dinner. White rice and white rice only.

As I watched her body continue to shrink over the semester, I felt like this *had* to be a marriage-related message from God. I was supposed to do this too. Hours at the gym. Bowls of white rice. I would have a husband by the end of the year.

The eternal partner part never materialized, but the rice-only diet seemed to finally work after a semester of eating only saltless, bland, blanched grain, each bowl consumed with a healthy dose of self-righteousness and heavenly optimism.

I have no idea how I managed to get good grades when caffeine was forbidden (God said so) and my diet didn't consist of anything other than starch, but I sure as hell did it. Much to my dismay, I never nabbed a Returned Missionary while in Rexburg, but I definitely lost *some* weight during those fall months.

The Summer Work Out and Starve Diet (Age Nineteen)

While spending a summer back in Tucson, I decided that the weight lost on my rice and Hannity diet wasn't quite enough, but without this designated food restriction I started to see my body fill out again. Without classes or any other obligations (damn, it's nice to live at home), I spent five to six hours every day at the gym near my grandmother's house. Running on the treadmill while watching *Friends* (a scandalous show for such a young Mormon—they talked about *sex* in it!) and then lifting weights with the Goo Goo Dolls blaring through my headphones on repeat ("Iris," if you must know), I was killing the weight-loss game. That combined with eating very little (proudly sharing with anyone who would listen how many kinds of foods I wasn't allowing myself to consume) continued to force my body to lose weight whether it was problematic or not.

It seemed almost inevitable for me—my life was literally exercising and dieting 24/7. And it "paid off." I returned to school and was met with "Oh my gosh, I hardly recognize you! You look so great!" and got to enjoy my first experience of being platonically noticed by a boy. Only one boy, but a real live boy.

It wasn't sustainable for me (or anyone?) in real life, and while I wasn't and never would be "that" thin again,[5] I did get a glimpse into what fat people who lose some weight—however temporarily—must feel like for a moment.

The praise was addicting. The lifestyle was alarming.

The Vodka Tonic and Capri Diet (Age Twenty-One)

I somehow managed to make clubbing a diet. Drinking nothing but vodka and tonics (vodka and soda, if I was feeling particularly self-righteous) and smoking slender Capris while I flirted with hipsters became my full-time job. My second job (forty hours a week, sure, but less important) as a bookstore employee added to my "cool cred" but was inconveniently located on the other side of town.

Broke (as someone who makes minimum wage and parties every night tends to be), I rode a bicycle an hour to and from work out of necessity (a car was too much of a responsibility), which allowed me to revel in my simplistic lifestyle that included not eating much during the day (you quickly learn that the less you eat the drunker you can get off of fewer drinks) and "exercising" on my way to work every day. If I did eat, I promptly threw it up. I knew my priorities, and food wasn't one of them.

I sadly look back on pictures from those days and see such a beautiful girl who couldn't have harmed or hated her body more.

5. Even at my smallest as an adult I was plus size and continuously devastated that I couldn't fit into the largest size of jeans they carried at American Eagle. Is American Eagle still a thing people care about?

The Melba Toast Diet (Age Twenty-Four)

Fully aware that my toxic relationship was failing, I decided that my body must be the problem. I proposed a solution to my then partner (who at that point wouldn't touch me) that I start eating nothing but melba toast (the internet promised this was a solid weight-loss plan) while taking Fen-Phen diet pills.

He agreed that this was an excellent idea, and I stuck to this diet for a grand total of thirty-six hours. That shit tasted worse than I imagine carpet would. I'm glad I left the diet behind, but I also should have left someone who encouraged this as a solution to our intimacy problems.

Fuck that dude.

The Lifestyle-Change Diet (Age Twenty-Six)

Trying to let go of my embarrassing past of carpet-eating, chalk-drinking, chemical-ingesting diets, I did what everyone else who was equally delusional and trying to accomplish the same thing did: I committed myself to a grand overhaul and lifestyle change.

I threw away everything in my cupboards, refrigerator, and freezer and replaced it with quinoa, kale, and frozen shots of wheatgrass. I bought a juicer, went to dehumanizing yoga classes, ate things I hated, and celebrated each moment of total misery. I gave myself a pat on the back for being such a "healthy person." Happiness would come later . . . right?

Restriction is restriction, guys, and the only constant found in my disturbing history of dieting is that it can't and won't work forever.

·········

So, have I ever thought about dieting?

All my life, man. I actively dieted like a fucked-up, beauty-obsessed champ for the majority of it. It did literally nothing to help me love or take care of myself. If anything, it did the opposite. I spent years feeling suicidal over the self-hatred that I continued to reinforce with every new fanatical attempt to change my body into something that others continued to demand. Diets can kiss my ass.

Got any other brilliant ideas?

CHAPTER 14

....

Maybe I'm a Hobbit?

I LOUNGED ON my aunt's bed like only a careless ten-year-old with no responsibilities or understanding of the real world could while she curled her hair in the bathroom, carefree and content while soaking in the luxury of a house that always had Costco-sized Pantene shampoo bottles (that came *with a pump*—key feature required). To me, a Suave kid afforded no other options, those bottles were extravagance in its purest form. I basked in the glow of opulence and mused aloud about how pleased I was that I didn't have any underarm hair and how I didn't plan on growing some anytime soon. She leaned out the doorway, curler in hand, and looked at me: "Just wait until you hit puberty, Jes. Everyone gets it."

"Nope," I sighed confidently, crossing one leg over my knee. It was clear to me that I was predestined to be special; a decade on this planet and not a single sign of armpit hair. "I think I'm gonna just skip it all together!" I called confidently in her direction. *It's nice to be me,* I thought. Leg switch and an arm stretch.

She didn't bother arguing about puberty with a fifth-grader, and I don't blame her.

Things I strongly believed at ten:

1. That I would eventually live in NYC so I would never have to drive, because cars were terrifying.

2. I would someday turn a hollowed-out tree into an underwear store.

3. Plan B, if the underwear store didn't work out, I would become a professional ballerina.

4. My underarms would stay soft and hairless.

5. My wisdom teeth would either never grow in or would never have to be pulled.

Things that are real life now that I'm thirty-one:

1. I just got a speeding ticket from being a defensive (read: asshole) driver while still living in Tucson. I still live on the opposite side of the country from NYC.

2. Because most hollowed-out trees don't meet building codes, the Berenstain Bear-esque panty store was apparently a Never Gonna Happen pipe dream.

3. Becoming a professional ballerina requires starting when you're three with a body I didn't have. Scratch out Plan B too.

4. My underarms are now naturally covered with thin, curly brown hair.

5. I've somehow avoided dental surgery.

Three cheers for those unobtrusive wisdom teeth; way to back me up, guys! I'm clinging to your absence, so do *not* let me down.

I've only achieved one out of five goals, and while 20 percent may look like a failure on paper, I'm so *not* sad about skipping teeth extraction, so I'll take that Pima County speeding ticket instead any day, thank you very much.

Even if I didn't know much as a ten-year-old, I certainly knew that hair growth was unladylike and beyond undesirable. (Imagine my surprise in my late teens when not so thin, not so curly, but definitely brown hair appeared on my *face*. *That* wasn't supposed to happen, not at all.) As a preteen I'd come to the conclusion that there was no way unwanted hair of any kind—but especially not facial hair—could be a part of my life (I'm not sure who is to blame for this except for beauty commercials I must have absorbed).

My childhood was saturated with Mormonism. Add to that puberty, the awkwardness of my horizontally growing body, and the fact that I was enrolled in G.A.T.E.,[1] along with being banned from ever wearing (what I *thought* was undetectable) mascara to school or anything slightly formfitting because Jesus said so . . . well, it was all more awkward than any preteen years ever should be. There wasn't much I could do to take control of my appearance.

On the bright side, I *was* allowed to have enormous bangs that were curled up and backward. (Imagine putting an aluminum soda can at the top of your forehead, brushing your four-inch bangs backward over it, using an entire bottle of hairspray to keep it in place, and then removing the can—voilà! Instant "Worst Hairstyles from the 90s" Tumblr fodder!)

I'm not sure why this extravagant hairstyle was allowed when everything else was off-limits. Maybe my mom subscribed to "the bigger the bangs, the higher to heaven" reasoning? I still don't know.

....

1. The popularity-crushing section of school that was for the "gifted kids," which at the time made me feel like I always had a nerd target on my back. But now I realize I was no victim but actually someone participating in a damaging differentiation made by a school as to whom they deemed intellectually special and who wasn't. Fuck that shit.

All of this is to say, there was no way in hell that I was ever going to be "pretty," and being cool was off the table too.

Unable to control myself, though, I channeled my rebellious side and decided that the perfect loophole to regain control of my body *without breaking* any of the makeup or clothing rules again was to take kid scissors to my astounding hair. I cut it in a way that was more or less rectifiable by a trip to Supercuts, but unfortunately the brand-new wispy sideburns that I had chopped remained.

Still aching to feel physically acceptable no matter the cost, when offered the chance to have a Glamour Shots photo session not long after the hair-cutting incident, I lost it. I probably shouted H-E-Double Hockey Sticks, YES![2] I immediately started practicing hand poses—should they be pulling at my bedazzled jacket collar? Or maybe just one hand resting against the side of my face? Would I look better if I rested my chin on my femininely posed hand, complete with a slightly raised finger? Uncool kids need hobbies too; this was mine for a month.

As I sat in the mall's swivel chair and looked into the mirror while the beautician started to apply the decade's appropriate amount of blush (easily summarized as *way too much*), I felt self-conscious about the sideburn-esque hair she was bound to see. Even at that age, I was aware that hair in the wrong places was revolting, a sign of something wrong.

To escape my worst fear of her noticing and judging silently, I felt compelled to confess what I had done. "I just want you to know," I said, pulling at the inch of hair that came down in front of my ear "My hair doesn't *actually* grow like this. I cut it myself, so . . . " She was clearly uninterested (about my hair and probably her mall job too) and replied, "Oh. Well, my friend has hair that grows just like that, so I didn't notice." As the emotional weight of worrying that

....
2. My childhood curse word substitutions are still a source of embarrassment.

a random adult would judge my hair lifted, I relaxed back into the chair. Peace only came when I knew that everyone in that room had been notified that I wasn't a hairy freak. She teased my hair into a gravity-defying pompadour and then enshrouded me in red tulle. I felt like there was a good chance they had Glamor Shots in heaven.

Today, when I look at those overly softened images of a thirteen-year-old wearing enormous geometric clip-on earrings, seventeen layers of foundation, and a purple smoky eye, posing as seductively as a seventh-grader could (I went with the chin propped up on my "delicate hand" pose) my thoughts are insuppressible:

1. DAMN, Aqua Net, way to come through. Even post–DIY scissor cut, I still had *so* much hair, and it was the tallest it's been in my life. Not just the bangs—all of it.

2. My second thought is and always will be, *Whoever thought this was a good idea for children was DEFINITELY a pervert.*

It's no surprise that I was worried about facial hair, though. Hair on one's face and the associated humiliation has been a part of my life for a long time, from first noticing a couple curious chin hairs on my mom as a child and the stubble on my aunt's neck to then dealing with my own unwanted stubbly sideburns followed by the shadow that eventually appeared on my chin and spread to my neck.

Our family was exceptionally talented when it came to denying the existence of anyone's facial hair. While I noticed facial hair on other members of our immediate and extended family, it was never mentioned, not even in hushed whispers or behind doors that I could press my ear against. The secrecy, along with a ubiquitously fat-hating world, had me counting each hair as it grew, blaming myself for this new and unwanted feature. I was firmly convinced that the reason chin hairs appeared was to serve as a reminder of my body-weight failure. I was certain that if I could just become thinner, they would disappear. I somehow came to believe body hair was the punishment that accompanied my fat body.

My body size became the target of all shame, regardless of its validity. If I hurt my back from carrying something too heavy, it happened because I was fat. If I had a rash on my arms from bug bites, the rash was caused by my fatness. I even believed that my lingering coughs were due to my weight.

It wasn't until my early twenties that I heard of polycystic ovary syndrome, or PCOS, a common diagnosis for many women with symptoms including weight gain, difficulty losing weight, thinning hair, and, yes, hormonal facial hair.

I took this (not novel to the rest of the world, but life-changing for me) revelation to my family and was met with a blasé, "Oh, yeah, most of us have that. It's genetic," from my grandma, my aunt, and my mom.

Why didn't anyone think to mention this while I was growing up? The amount of shame that I had been carrying around lessened considerably. The hair was still as exasperating as ever, but at least I didn't have to shoulder the fabricated guilt along with the upsetting cheek moss.

Even after becoming aware that my thickening sideburns weren't a sign of moral failure, PCOS continued to control my entire life. From rejecting the soothing hair wash that comes before a haircut (God forbid my hair stylist's fingers get anywhere near the stubble near my ears) to only talking to my coworkers while facing them directly so they would have less of an opportunity to notice, I would do almost anything to hide my hideously hairy features from the world. If I knew that I would be driving with someone, I would focus my shaving and plucking on the side that would face them, hoping the sunlight wouldn't highlight my quickly growing five o'clock shadow. I went from wondering if everyone who stared at me was looking at my tattoos, outrageous clothing, or size to wondering if my chin beard was visible to the person behind me in Starbucks.

I let it control my love life, finding myself single and thinking, *I reeeeeally don't want to have a serious partner right now because I reeeeeally don't want to have to worry about facial hair all the time.* I craved love, but I craved the safety of physical distance that allowed me to hide my facial hair more.

Every morning I shaved with a men's razor (pro tip: closer shave!) and cream. I tried Nair, the creepy coils with pink ends, and every other home contraption you could purchase at Walgreens. I shaved every morning (and twice a day if I had somewhere to be at night). I perfected a hair-removing Netflix routine where I would prop myself up on one elbow, the other hand feeling for hair and tweezing while watching *Lost*. One episode per side was all I needed to feel considerably more confident. I secretly prided myself on this streamlined and effective performance. Second pro tip: Spending an hour in the car during the day to tweeze is particularly effective, as sunlight has the amazing ability to show you just how many hairs you have. Note: This is not for the faint of heart.

Hyper self-conscious, I often refused to let my date caress my face or kiss my neck, even though there are not many things I find as hot. When I finally decided to choose a relationship over my impressively stubborn stubble, I found myself in the very situation I had always feared: my new partner stroked my face one time in the beginning, noticeably pulling away. After the abrupt but silent retraction, not a word was said, but we both knew the reason. I was aware of my monstrous secret, and now they were too. Several years into our relationship, even until the bitter end, we never talked about this symptom of PCOS.

Until last year, I had never talked about this with a lover.

Ever.

I wrote about my hormone discovery on the internet once, but I never spoke a word about it to the people who were all up in my personal space, waking up to me every morning; the people who inevitably saw me in every state of my physical existence. I continued to pretend that PCOS was not part of my life, even when I was around the people that I couldn't hide it from.

It was impossible to ignore, but God knows I tried.

I feel like Kristen Wiig's *Bridesmaids* character and I might be the same person.

The opening scene shows Kristen's mess of a character, Annie Walker, waking up next to the conventionally attractive Ted, the dude she sleeps with for validation, among other things.[3] She glances over as he continues to snore, and then she slides out of bed and runs into the bathroom. She reapplies makeup, spritzes perfume, shapes her hair, and then tiptoes back to bed, sliding under the covers unnoticed. As Ted wakes up and turns toward her, she performs a perfect stretch and yawn. It couldn't be clearer that she woke up this way.

I've secretly performed a similar routine for years, except for one difference: I wasn't applying makeup—I was shaving my face. Slipping out of bed, sneaking into the bathroom, shaving as fast and as closely as I could, and then sliding back under the covers, finally semi-comfortable with being seen.

Pretending you don't have facial hair is kind of like being fat, wearing black, and expecting it to suddenly make you thinner. It doesn't fool anyone. You're still gonna be fat, and everyone is still gonna know.[4]

....

3. See Chapter 9, part 2 for further proof that Annie Walker and I are *definitely* poor decision-making twins.

4. Wear those colors and large prints, bb. It's all the same.

I wasn't fooling anyone with my early-morning shave routine and pretend yawns, but it was the best I could do. A solid eight hours of sleep left plenty of time for a significant amount of growth, and how was I supposed to have morning sex when I knew I had a beard? Between this, the massive pubic maintenance required to not grow an impenetrable hedge, cracked heels I've had since I was eight, dark underarm coloring, and moss sprouting on each of my toes, I was basically a hobbit, and I've never seen a hobbit have sex.[5]

It's really exhausting to try to hide the fact that you're a hobbit when you're trying really hard to be an elf queen. Really, really exhausting.

It was only last year, after waking up next to Andy for over 1095 days (I might have funded the razor market single-handedly; you're welcome, Gillette), that I decided to reveal the obvious but *terrifying* truth to my partner.

We were watching *Cutthroat Kitchen*. It was a nightly routine and one of those things that had taken us a while to sort out. Because of my undying love for fast-paced political thrillers and his contrasting affection for anything depressing and set in the slow Midwest . . . well, watching experienced chefs acting like toddlers in the name of $25,000 was one of the only shows that fell into our overlapping Netflix "Venn diagram" section, and Alton Brown was someone we both could, y'know, stand.[6]

---

5. That's a lie. I'm pretty certain that there were mirrors on the bedroom ceiling of one of my one-night stands.

6. Let it be known, though, that while we *tolerate* Alton, we are both so in love with Justin Warner that a threesome is never out of the question. Justin, just putting it out there, you know where to find us.

Fortunately between *Cutthroat Kitchen* and the *Kid's Baking Championship*,[7] there are more than a dozen seasons to love/hate watch. He's a cook and I'm a baker (we yell a lot at the TV, and it works), so I'm not gonna fight it.

We sat next to each other holding hands, my head on his shoulder, and while he serenely watched a grown-ass man try to prep food while in a McDonald's-style ball pit, my mind was distracted, trying to think of the best way to approach the obvious.

I took a deep breath and uttered the most obvious yet terrifying six words I had never strung together before. "Hey, babe? I have facial hair." I couldn't bear to look at him, so I stared straight ahead, pretending that watching a smug chef try to cook on a wobbling boat was the most riveting thing I had ever seen. "I know," he said softly. I mean, I knew he knew (I'm aware of my inability to con someone who sleeps next to me for three years straight), but I was still surprised at his stunningly neutral answer. I wasn't satisfied. Andy is one of the most brilliant people I know, and this didn't add up; he *clearly* didn't get the repulsiveness that I had just stated. I needed to reiterate the issue so he could understand. "Okay. But it's really unsexy." My voice faltered as I named another correlated and unspoken fear. "Well," he turned to smile at me, "there are less sexy things in the world, y'know."

I nestled my head on his arm, for the first time comfortable with letting my cheek touch someone else's skin. There is so much power in naming your monsters. And there is so much safety in a partner who loves all of you.

I stopped running into the bathroom every morning and feigning my wakeups. I shaved at night before bed and called it good enough. And while I still stood in the bathroom and closely

---

7. Why are crying children so entertaining? Every episode makes me wonder if we are horrible people.

inspected my face after a long day of work, bemoaning the inevitable stubble, the self-imposed hair hatred that I brought into our relationship was gone.

Eventually, I saw some hateful comments online surmising, "I think she has a beard," but at that point there was no longer a reason to hide.[8] Blowing the shame door wide open, I shared a mirror selfie with shaving cream covering the lower half of my face with the caption "When that PCOS life is real AF." This simple image spurred hundreds of comments from readers who had also been living the same hair-hiding life. We'd all been feeling like we were the only ones who suffered from same steadfast humiliation, but we were no longer alone.

It's a special feeling, sharing your secret with the world and then coming home to a place where anxiety about PCOS symptoms is no longer welcome. There is a strange phenomenon that happens when you speak your greatest fears or most shameful thoughts out loud. I've often heard this act of courage compared to a virus. If a virus has a bodily host, it can continue to thrive. However, if you expose that same virus to air? It dies upon contact. I have found this to be a powerful biological analogy when it comes to sharing our excruciatingly vulnerable feelings with our friends, partner, and, yes, even the internet.

And while sharing my liberation with the world felt wonderful, I am most grateful for a *home* where there are no unspoken fears and I am allowed to enter and *just be*.

---

8. I *did* contemplate shaving my back for the book cover shoot. That's still a real thing.

CHAPTER 15

....

In Praise of Loud and Fat Women

SOME OF THE most influential moments I've had in untangling my identity as a fat woman didn't come from reading theories and how-to lists about body image—how to find self-empowerment or why flipping off the status quo is important. They contributed, absolutely, but I dare say that one of the most potent pieces of my introduction to fat-girl survival came from watching the experiences and even the endurance of loud and fat women throughout my life.

These women did everything: horrified me, emboldened me, educated me, and gave me uncomfortable spaces to sit in as well as permission to not only exist, but also turn my existence into something magnificent.

And while their unapologetic fatness was a raucous and rallying war cry in and of itself, they also roared in other ways, each an individual inspiration in their refusal to shrink silently as the world demanded they do.

1) Beth Ditto

Bookmans is the most hallowed bookstore in Tucson.

After escaping Brigham Young University–Idaho and religion as a whole by returning home for the summer when I turned twenty, I was offered a job at this used-book emporium, the most coveted place of employment for every narcissistic hipster in the state.

It was the size of a confusingly large department store, run by the most apathetic (hence: cool) group of misfits you could find.[1] People literally made a point to stop in Tucson to shop its sacred shelves of previously read and resold chick-lit paperbacks, *MAD* and *Travel Life* magazines, astronomy textbooks, and seemingly endless copies of *Marley and Me* that we could never seem to stock fast enough.

I often worked opposite the registers on the "trade counter," an endless surface where customers could drop off piles of everything from books to vintage melamine cups to boxes of trinkets in exchange for a yellow slip of paper containing "Bookmans credit." Once, we even took items from a woman who set her box down on the counter and promptly announced to everyone within earshot that she had just been diagnosed with MRSA. Went through that box too (we wore gloves).

One afternoon, a coworker named Miguel (known for repeatedly calling the store from the front counter until I answered and then, posing as an anonymous customer, asking me to find and read the titles of every book we had on the shelf about the Kama Sutra. It took me three times to catch on) was leafing through a magazine. He shouted for me to come over and look at something.

....
1. It's worth noting that the manager informed me after offering me the job that he almost declined my application after my interview because I was too "cheerful." Fear not, though! Within six months I had become the disillusioned degenerate every Bookmans employee aims to be!

He grinned as he presented me with the table of contents of *Bust* magazine, an image of the growling lead singer of the band Gossip, Beth Ditto, posing for the world on the sidebar. Her extravagant outfit and confident stance was lost on me as he said, "You look just like her!"

I was horrified and humiliated. I saw nothing but a socially reviled fat body that absolutely *couldn't* look like mine. I was still deeply entrenched in my body-loathing days, trying to ignore my size whenever possible. But I couldn't pretend my body didn't exist in that moment; Miguel saw *me* in *this* picture and was holding it out so not only I could see but also everyone else in the vicinity. His smile showed that he obviously thought he was paying me a compliment,[2] but I angrily said, "Fuck you, I look NOTHING like that." A few female coworkers agreed, attempting to show solidarity in my fear of being fat.

Truth be told, I *was* smaller than Beth at the time, and I clutched on to whatever body currency I had and held it tightly, unwilling to ease my grip at all. I mentally pushed the magazine and the comparison as far away as possible for years until I discovered the magical world of not hating your body years later.

And still, while I shunned Beth Ditto that day, she was the first fierce, fat, and fabulous woman I had ever laid my eyes on. She represented a group of people I didn't know existed. She was sweaty and unapologetic, wore gold bodysuits, and was the ferocious lead singer of a phenomenal band.

It should be noted that I unabashedly dressed as Beth Ditto for Halloween a few years later, now savvy to how appropriate it was to worship the fat-positive poster girl for an unruly and misfit group of women who felt like they had nowhere else to fit in.

Nearly ten birthdays and five years of online body-image activism later, I found myself a keynote speaker at a plus-size fashion

....
2. To be honest, he was. Beth Ditto is a superbabe.

show in Portland, Oregon, hurling profanity and praising the politics of fatshion, with Beth herself in the audience, the people around her cheering in solidarity.

Playing the "No, I won't be the person who begs for a picture with you" game after the event ended, I mingled with friends until I ended up in the same circle as this woman who I had distanced myself from with incredible detestation years ago.

It didn't take long before she came over herself, hugging me and exclaiming "I LOVE YOU!" as I hugged her back (fully aware of the amount of sweat that had dried into body odor—thanks synthetic, sweat-accumulating mesh). I realized that the tables had turned.

Turned as in: I was now legitimately the size of her body as it had been in the table of contents years ago, and she had lost a significant amount of weight (she never talked about this, but the media did not fail to notice) since that issue and was more the size of "Volatile Bookmans Jes."

We had traded bodies, but because of her—the first radically unapologetic fat woman I had seen in the media—this was perfectly okay with me. Her music, her leotards, her memoir, her fiery existence had created a mental space in which being a fat babe was possible.

Beth Ditto was the reason I was there at that particular event. She's the reason I'm still here in this world.

God bless that Gossip girl. Not only for showing me the first path I'd seen toward loud and unapologetic body acceptance, but also for hugging me when I smelled so bad that even I desperately wanted to take a few steps away from myself.

2) Rachele Cateyes

Before I had the bravery to dress as Beth Ditto for Halloween, I often spent nights tirelessly blog hopping, following one sidebar recommendation after another, enjoying the polished images and content that reminded me of magazines, only way cooler. I will never forget the night that I stumbled across The Nearsighted Owl, written by Rachele.

This blog baffled me. It had all the components I loved—recipes, owls, polka dots, and purple beehives—but with one difference. Rachele was fat. She was not only fat—she was fat, confident, and happy. How. The. Fuck. Does. That. Happen? Scrolling through her posts, my mind was momentarily broken, trying to wrap itself around the fact that there was a woman in the world who looked nothing like the "ideal" but was living a full and joyous life. No shame, no apologies, only confident posts about her favorite books, her art projects, her marriage (this is where I discovered that fat people get married too!), and her heroes.

I continued to visit the page out of genuine curiosity, and soon I was hit with the most revolutionary thought: Maybe I don't have to loathe myself for the rest of my life.

Maybe I don't have to loathe myself for the rest of my life!

Maybe I can even sort of . . . like myself! Could it be true?

Well, if Rachele can do it, perhaps . . . yeah. Maybe I can too! It's astounding to me that I hadn't realized this before. But, fuck. I'm glad that I did at age twenty-six. Better late than never, right? After discovering Rachele, I dove headfirst into the body-positive community. I sought out photos of all kinds of women, I followed progressive Tumblr accounts, and I read every fat-acceptance book I could get my chubby hands on. I read all the body-love blogs I could find, researched the history of body image, and started to talk about all of this with people around me.

Though she doesn't blog in the same way any longer, she continues to flood the internet with forceful artwork that contains sentiments like "Fat people don't owe you shit" and a drawing of ten middle fingers that border the words "Your opinion of my health."

She shaved her head, documents "unflattering" outfits, and literally does not give a shit about what you think about her. In person, she is quiet and shy. She mentions that social anxiety keeps her in the comfort of her home more often than not. But none of that changes the fact that she is a fierce and formidable force to be reckoned with in every way.

3) Margie Ashcroft

A clothing company contacted me a few days after my first "viral" photo shoot landed me on the *Today* show and invited me to a plus-size pop-up shop in NYC.

I had been blogging long enough to know who was part of the fatshion elite and that they would all be there. As I walked into this invite-only event with wide eyes, donning a bizarrely altered dress and my dirty, worn-out cowboy boots, my novice status was obvious. The round tables were filled with poised fashionistas who looked like they were leaving the event and flying to have tea with the goddamn Queen of England.[3] I stuck out like a sore, clumsy, and crude thumb. Let's not mince words. Not only am I a naturally loud person vocally, but my ensemble spoke volumes as well. It was pretty obvious I had no idea what I was doing.

The presentation of the plus line consisted of a thin woman in a cityscape dress and their plus-size tailor, who looked magical in her galaxy fit and flare.[4] They explained their production process and said something about how they made their own patterns to send since no one knew how to dress a fat body, and while everyone else politely clapped I heard a shrill "HOLLA!" from the back corner.

....
3. Which, for some, was a complete possibility.

4. Does anyone else still love galaxy print on everything five years later? No? Just me?

I turned to see a platinum-haired girl with bright red lipstick in an electric-blue top grinning. A wave of relief washed over me. I wasn't the only rowdy weirdo here. She later introduced herself as Margie, and it became obvious that she was loud as fuck and proud of it.

That night, we plus-sized fashion weirdos united under a rainbow disco ball while belting out NSYNC lyrics, loving the fact that we were nearly trampled by a crowd of people even more fabulous than the two of us.

You can find her online wearing hot-pink sunglasses. She rocks high-waisted shorts that gather in between her legs—something most people avoid. She will yell across a room without an ounce of embarrassment. Her laugh can be heard above everyone else's. She now has neon-esque yellow hair. She embodies every aspect of loud and gives permission to those around her to do the same.

4) Sonya Renee Taylor

There are four things I will *never* forget about the first time I met Sonya:

1. She agreed to be a speaker in our first-ever Tucson body-image conference, and the night before we went to dinner at a conference sponsor's restaurant, which specialized in fish entrees. I sat across from her at the dinner table as she skimmed the menu with a disdainful look. "I never trust fish served in a landlocked state," she said resolutely. I chuckled as an Arizonan who always appreciated the options and watched with a smile as she ordered something else; I couldn't tell you what it was, but it for damn sure wasn't something from the ocean.

2. When she presented (to a standing room–only crowd), she wore what I can only assume is her "power dress": a color-blocked maxi with several different shades of blue and a dramatic yellow V-neck highlighting the other colors. There

was something about the way she carried herself in that vibrant ensemble. Her baldness, her bold colors, her confidence. . . . I couldn't help but hear the roar she never uttered.

3. The moment when she asked each audience member to raise their hand if they had ever participated in a diet. The majority raised their hands without hesitation. She then explained that she was going to start at age thirty and count down; if you were on a diet at the age she called out, you were to leave your hand in the air. She started counting down: *Thirty. Twenty-five. Twenty. Fifteen.* Slowly, hands were dropped, but I remained astounded at the number of people who still had their arms raised.

    Ten. Nine. Eight. Seven. Still, multiple hands remained up, representing their dieting history. *Six. Five. Four.* The last woman held her hand high. She had been dieting since prekindergarten. The crowd, covered in goosebumps and filled with obvious sorrow, applauded in solidarity for this person, someone who had been taken advantage of by diet culture before even hitting elementary school. Sonya radiated love toward her; it was one of the most powerful examples of the realities of body shaming. To this day, this activity has remained with me as one of the most heart-wrenching and clarifying reasons that body-image advocates engage in this work.

    There is one picture ingrained in my memory from that lecture: a photo of me leaning against the wall hysterically laughing at an obviously comedic moment—my most radiant self has never been so perfectly captured. This is the power she brings out in everyone she meets.

4. Still in the beginnings of my "body-advocate days," I was able to have a conversation with Sonya, who by all means had had

every opportunity to internalize bitterness, anger, and hatred in a world that refused to ensure her safety and in fact actively worked toward her erasure. I expected and would have welcomed this angry attitude, aware of the fact that it was beyond understandable.

Instead, I was met with a discussion full of compassion, global love, and forgiveness. Over the years, Sonya has taught me more about the importance of public education, the extensive importance of body acceptance, and the critical personal capacity to hone resiliency skills than anyone else.

If the world was on fire (which, arguably, it kinda is) and I could only choose one person to save for the next version of civilization, it would undoubtedly be Sonya, because the next civilization is going to need her.

5) Lindy West

The reason so many people hate her was the reason I fell in love. Someone once said that when she writes it's as if she climbs on top of a school desk, throws her arms in the air, and yells, "MY NAME IS LINDY WEST AND I AM RIGHT!⁵"

Anyways. In *my* world, Lindy West is in an empty classroom, standing (in a mid-length floral-print dress with puffy long sleeves—I don't know why this is important) on the seat of a graphite-gouged wooden student desk with green trim, and is roaring IMPORTANT FUCKING FACT after IMPORTANT FUCKING FACT at the top of her lungs. To who? It doesn't matter. They're important fucking facts, and Lindy is yelling them right now.

....

5. They left out the school desk and arm throwing part, but I like my version better.

There is something reverent about imagining a grown-ass woman in a seventies floral dress yelling things that people in your past life have only whispered about.

It gives you the permission you need to stop whispering for once. Everyone needs a polyester-donning desk yeller in their life. Lindy West is mine.

6) Mary Lambert

First person I saw play a normal fat love interest in a music video: Mary Lambert.

First person to write a pop song with the lyrics "I've got bipolar disorder, my shit's not in order": Mary Lambert.

First person to radiate such calm and healing energy that it made me feel like I had just taken four milligrams of Xanax simply by standing next to her: Mary Lambert.

First person I've legitimately lost my shit over meeting and tried really hard to pretend I wasn't fangirling over so I just acted like a loud, bossy brat and I'm *still* embarrassed by it: Mary Lambert.

First person I know of who publicly normalizes fatness and mental illness and paves the way for me to shamelessly do the same: Mary Lambert.

First person I lent a swimsuit to while in Dallas: Ashley Nell Tipton.[6] Mary Lambert got the second one. Did you know I never washed that swimsuit again?[7]

First person who showed me how extraordinary softness can sometimes be the most powerful catalyst for radical change: Mary Lambert.

....

6. This was never intended to include awkward humble brags, but I'm human, so here we are.

7. That's a lie. I washed it, wore it in Belize, and then almost immediately lost it, which is a bummer because it highlighted my chest tattoos perfectly.

First person I fell in love with at first sight: Probably my mom, but we're gonna go with Mary Goddamn Lambert.

7) Ijeoma Oluo

> "Ijeoma! I'm in Seattle for the next day and THIS IS BOLD BUT I'd love to take you out to breakfast/brunch/early lunch tomorrow . . . if you're into that kind of thing and available."

I sat back and reread the Twitter message I had just swipe-typed seventeen times. Was it too forward? Did I spell everything right? There were thirty-four words, which meant there were thirty-four chances to fuck this up. Was the offer too presumptuous? Was it offensive to ask to "take someone out"? Was Twitter a weird way to contact a legendary luminary? *Did she even know who I was? Would I regret this message for the rest of my life?*

For someone who publicly misspells something in almost every status going out to 140,000 people weekly, I put *a lot* of effort into a message only one person would see.

I stopped my mental spiraling long enough to click Send and promptly had a mild panic attack. Then, I checked my account obsessively.

The three hundred and seventh time made my insides drop several feet inside me. A check mark appeared. *She had read it.* Four seconds ago. But there wasn't a reply yet. Was I now officially a horrible person? Should I just quit my online job all together? Was my value as a human now obsolete?

A short message appeared a few minutes later: "I'd love to. I should be available after 10 a.m. or so"

I was breathing again, but still concerned. No period. Did that mean that she had hastily typed it because of complete indifference?

Or was it because she was in a hurry, on her phone, and checking an impersonal social media platform?

Positive that it was most likely the first, I quickly used my thumbs to reply.

"YAYAYAYAYYAY" I sent back enthusiastically, regret settling in immediately. Nonpunctuated responses should *not* be replied to with such transparent fanaticism. God, Jes, *get a grip. It was* only *Ijeoma Oluo.*

But I couldn't, because of that same reason: I had just messaged IJEOMA OLUO. I had just invited my favorite writer and human on the internet to sit at the same table with me, and if I'm going to be entirely honest, I was terrified by what I had just done. She was, after all, one of the most brilliant people on this planet, if not in this galaxy. Not only because every word she wrote was a psalm the world wasn't worthy of, but also because when she claps back at ego-clutching assholes, everyone can feel the entire Earth shake.

It took a lot of bravery (maybe derangement?) to offer to eat breakfast food across from someone you not only admired but who also had a brain that could effortlessly run circles around yours.

After agreeing on a time and place, I made a reservation over the phone, both distracted and amazed by the likely life-altering meal that would happen in less than twenty-four hours. Before leaving the houseboat I was staying in (yes, jealousy is an appropriate response to this), I triple-checked my Uber time estimate so I wasn't late. Once I arrived at the restaurant, I waited near the door as it rained in true Seattle fashion. She never showed up.

Fuck. *I knew this was a terrible idea.*

I had her number and gave myself pep talks until I was brave enough to use it. "Here whenever you are!" A string of texts and apologies for showing up at the wrong location came back, and I let out an audible sigh of relief. My hero-worshiping relaxed; she was human too. Thank GOD.

Brunch turned out to be lovely. She walked in—much taller than I imagined—wearing a red dress that radiated casual but stunning confidence, with a stride that mirrored the same. We ordered everything delicious on the menu, which included a book-noteworthy *French toast bar.*

We chatted about her children; her youngest had a YouTube channel that I wished I remembered the name of because it sounded adorable. We also talked about normal things that I was prepared for social-justice writers to converse about: Seattle's housing crisis, our upcoming books, the joy of petty blocking, and why she never wants to write about racism again but knows that she must.

The ease of the date reminded me of a truth that I usually remembered in every instance besides this: we're all just humans. Each with a life full of different stories and talents, sure, but at the end of the day? We're all equally mortal.

Following this (very much *not* scary) brunch, we had future conversations over Skype that were meant to last thirty minutes but went on for hours. I loved every second. This monumental figure that I saved a significant amount of my (limited) respect for was not only fierce and, yes, intellectually intimidating but was *also* beautifully vulnerable and empathetic.

These seamless and authentic coalescing traits taught me another truth I already knew but occasionally forget: you can be both soft and tough, and these attributes aren't necessarily incompatible.

Ijeoma was the illuminated personification of my favorite line from the poet Nayyirah Waheed: "i am a brutally soft woman."

Boldness and vulnerability can *and do* live together peacefully, and as a fat woman in this world, this is something I strive to achieve every day. Ijeoma lives it daily, through her online presence and by unknowingly continuing to encourage me simply by living her authentic truth.

Honestly, there are hundreds of people who belong on this list, along with every single fat woman who enjoys food in public, wears something she feels sexy in, makes a small smile when she walks by a mirror, or simply wears joy on her face. Each time I see these things, it reinforces the fact that fat women are some of the most beautiful, radiant, and resilient creatures on the planet.

They continually give me permission and reminders that I can fully inhabit my existence. Not regardless of my size, but because of it.

Loud and fat women are whom I have to thank for the unleashing of my own voice. They have given me permission to use that voice. They have paved the way to make space for that voice as well as given me the knowledge that loudness and fatness are a combination that can change the world no matter what form it takes.

We're not sorry if you're starstruck, and you can totally blame it on the stardust.[8] Can't you see our fucking crowns?

8. Kesha's song *Hymn* gets it, and if you know what I mean, you're on the team.

CHAPTER 16

David and Goliath

A FEW SUN RAYS bent across my sheets, streaming through my cat-battered blinds, as my phone "pinged" as an incoming text announced that everyone else I knew was awake and facing the world except for me. I pushed my pillows down, rolled over, and fumbled for my phone.

It was a message from Paula, a friend who has a charming habit of keeping me updated on every article related to body image that shows up on the internet, especially during times of my life when I'm trying like hell to avoid the constant barrage of news. This was one of those times. It was a link to a *People* article, newly released, about celebrity-status, purple-haired, plus-size fashion designer Ashley Nell Tipton.

I scanned through the article, looking for the reason Paula might have sent it to me. The title had it all in one go: "Project Runway Winner Ashley Nell Tipton Reveals She Had Gastric Bypass Surgery Last Month." I turned off my phone screen, set it down next to my headphones (Yes, I fall asleep to Jim Dale's dulcet tones every night. Doesn't everyone?), and groaned.

My head still felt heavy and my vision was blurred, but I could feel—almost hear, even—dozens of body-image bloggers, journalists, and Facebook users sprinting to their computers across the country, all with the same biting and salt-saturated opinion stated in various ways: *Fat woman fails entire world again for getting weight-loss surgery and should be sent to the gallows for perilous moral ineptitude.*

I knew what the articles would say before they were written, but I still had questions about the consensus that would inevitably be published far and wide. Who had Ashley really failed? Herself? Her closest friends? A single person? A group of strangers in a Facebook group? The world at large? And just how far into intentional weight loss did a fat lady need to go to become a monumental failure? Where was the line wherein a fat woman would no longer have the support of her fat peers? How much weight does a fat lady need to lose to have her Fat Card revoked?

I pulled my covers over my head, made a mental note to never go on the internet again, and half-assedly kicked my feet in useless frustration. There was no way I was going to be able to go back to sleep.

God, I *really* hate mornings.

………

The previous May, I found myself sitting in waist-high grass, my head snuggled on Andy's shoulder, our faces turned to one of the most magnificent sunsets I've seen. We sat in silence while the sun slowly slid behind the calm oceanic horizon, and we listened to the waves crashing near us onto the coast of Big Sur. It was meditative. It was tranquil. It truly was perfect.

It was also one of the *only* "perfect" moments we'd had on that road trip down the coast of California.[1]

....

1. Note to all: If your partner's brain is naturally antisocial and short-circuits when faced with chaotic crowds, California is *not* the ideal travel destination.

We had left our excursion fairly open-ended, only planning a few stops, including the Monterey Bay Aquarium and an overpriced drink at the Madonna Inn, both of which, while worthwhile, were already pushing his social capacities. Despite his hesitations about waiting in line for the elephant seals or five-star tacos, I had somehow managed to convince him that going to Universal Studios was a *great* idea, full of fun, real magic, and probably less traumatizing than Disneyland. My luck in interesting him in this theme park can likely be credited in large part to the fact that we had been listening to Harry Potter audiobooks the entire drive. Or perhaps he was just feeling a little adventurous; either way, I didn't ask or care. *I was going to Harry Potter Land. I was going to touch Hogwarts.* I immediately booked tickets from the passenger seat for the next day the second he conceded with a resigned "Well, okay." I didn't fuck around when selecting our tickets for the wizarding experience of a lifetime. Front of the line, early entry, all-access pass. I was feeling what could only be described as total elation.

Feeling pumped beyond belief, I cranked back up the audiobook we were listening to[2] and reclined with a contented grin as we continued to drive. We took an exit shortly after our Universal Studio agreement to make one of our many drugstore stops (he always needs Tums and I always forget to bring gel insoles. We are basically eighty-year-olds in thirty-year-old bodies), and I sat in the Rite Aid lot while he darted inside. Unable to control my excitement over convincing my super-introverted partner (who obviously has a heavy handful of Hufflepuff tendencies) to visit an *amusement park*, I texted a friend who lived in LA to share that tomorrow I would be *in Hogsmeade* and she should be jealous as hell because BUTTERBEER. She quickly texted back: "Just so you know, we're the same size, and I didn't fit into any of the rides there."

....

2. *Harry Potter and the Prisoner of Azkaban*, obviously because it's the best one.

My sensitive and prideful (obviously Gryffindor) heart broke into a million grief-stricken pieces. I had just purchased an all-access pass to a wizarding escape from the real world, and now I was finding out there was a significant chance that I would be turned away before experiencing any magic at all. This thought was not something that had ever crossed my mind. My unchecked size privilege had slapped me hard across my face, and while it was well deserved, it still stung like hell. I slowly placed my phone back in my lap, absorbing this truth.

What do you mean I might not fit into the ride?

I've traveled. I've ridden Disneyland rides. I can stretch the hell out of body-con dresses the world randomly labeled as two sizes too small for me and pull it over my fat body. I was finally facing something that many fat people have had to deal with their entire lives. My size, while always an emotional life barrier, as of this very moment had at last become a solid physical barrier, a literal blockage between me and something I desperately wanted to do.

I had eked along for years, enjoying the unearned luxury of fitting into Target's plus-sized clothing,[3] most restaurant chairs, and only one airplane seat without getting a cynical look from flight attendants if I was careful to dramatically press my body against the cabin wall with a visible look of repentance. I had become accustomed to being fat enough to suffer through society's general harassment, but still "accommodated by lots of spaces in this world" fat. Perhaps I wasn't welcomed kindly to the table, and maybe there were loud and insulting whispers of fat jokes when I walked in the door, but I could still somehow manage to squish myself into a seat alongside others. I fully realized how lucky I was and yet still couldn't fathom that *this ride* was a public experience that I couldn't do.[4]

....

3. Well, some. Fuck you, rayon dresses.

4. This was a much-needed and deserved reminder of the extraordinary fat privilege I still had, even while living in a fatphobic society. This doesn't even begin to cover my other unearned privileges.

All of the old blame I had learned to feel about my body washed over me until I could think of nothing else. My body *had* to fit. It must fit. Because if it didn't, I was a worthless person. I would simply have to make it fit. This was clearly the only option.

Stunned and unable to move little more than my hands, I picked my phone back up and, without questioning myself, typed "lap band surgery" into my search engine. It felt like the most rational course of action in that moment. I researched the different options. The possible side effects. The horror and success stories. I will not deny that I often wonder if I "should" participate in weight-loss surgery. After all, it's sanctioned by so many anti-fat people. How could millions of fans be wrong? *Maybe,* I thought, *I didn't need to be strong anymore. Maybe I just needed to get this procedure done. Maybe it was finally time.*

Andy returned to the car, and as he got in I quickly clicked out of my browser with a different kind of shame creeping up on me—my inner fat-acceptance advocate clicking her tongue in disappointment[5] at my instantaneous willingness to compromise my anti–diet culture ethics and jump to weight-loss surgery as a solution. In an effort to atone for my moral lapse into old thinking, I decided to use the internet another way. "Hey, fat babes, have you flown on the Forbidden Journey, and did you fit? I've been reading mixed reviews and would love to know your experiences," I asked my followers. The comments I got in response were confusing at best. A size 22 fit, but a size 18 didn't. People with broad shoulders had difficulty, but people with bellies were actually the ones with the biggest chance of not being able to ride. The unpredictability reinforced something every larger-bodied person already knows: standardized sizing doesn't exist for us. At all.

....

5. That's a lie. She doesn't believe in holding back and actually gave me the finger.

Baffled and disappointed in both myself and the outcome of my ask, I collected whatever amount of rationality I had left and decided that the amount of time and emotional energy we would spend potentially waiting in line for a ride I might not fit on was a terrible waste when there were other ways to explore Los Angeles.

Because life is occasionally undeniably cruel, our "better way to spend time in Los Angeles" consisted of Andy's sleeping for days in our Airbnb host's bed sick with the flu. I tried passing the time but eventually decided to just nap it out, too. It became obvious that our moment on Big Sur and the amazing pink wingback chairs at the Madonna Inn were going to be the only highlights of our five-day trip.

Tucking the feeling of failure about being too fat to fly on Harry's Forbidden Journey as far back into my mind as I could, we returned the rental car and spent $25 to upgrade to first class on the flight home, during which we drank vodka at 7:30 in the morning to dull the pain and celebrate the ending of our hell of a road trip.

A few months later, I found myself in Los Angeles again with six extra hours after delivering a college lecture that left me burning with the need to do *something* audacious. I texted Bevin, a friend who had recently relocated to LA: "WANT TO GO TO UNIVERSAL STUDIOS WITH ME? Someone told me I couldn't ride the Harry Potter ride and now I HAVE to know."

My phone chimed almost instantly: "I'm up for anything!"

Bevin is basically a glorious, 5'7" piece of clarifying rose quartz in the shape of a fat, super queer, platinum blonde who wears enormous falsies and heals the shit out of any emotional wounds that those around her may have. It is not uncommon to lean in for a hug while feeling upset about something and then, the second after you are enveloped in her arms, to feel weightless and find yourself thinking: "Holy fuck. All of a sudden I feel a deep sense of personal fulfillment and am flooded with divine loving energy!"

Though she'll remind you often that she is a self-identified Gryffindor (and I don't doubt this), it is easier to describe her appearance and energy as a glitter-covered Luna Lovegood.

Y'know, if Luna Lovegood was shaped like Lumpy Space Princess and instead of Dirigible plum-shaped earrings she wore enormous rhinestone chandeliers. They both somehow glide instead of walk, remain calm in situations where others completely fall apart, and wear bold colors while speaking in soft tones. In short, she is an indescribably tender force of nature and was the perfect partner for this social experiment.

I hopped in an absurdly expensive Lyft (worth it because the driver blared Beyoncé), peeked into her adorable bungalow filled with Dolly Parton paraphernalia (also: pets!), and then we were off to answer the unanswerable: Will Jes Baker fit into Harry Potter and the Forbidden Journey?

Walking into Universal Studios, I was astounded at how detailed the efforts were to transport you out of reality and into another world. Did they have a "Childhood Freedom"–scented perfume that they sprayed in every corner to accompany the atmospheric music, which made you feel like maybe this was your real life but mostly you were a character in a Universal Studios movie? I was impressed. I couldn't help but become more and more excited with each swell of the orchestra in the background.

Dedicated to our mission, we headed straight toward Hogwarts Castle, its towers visibly reaching far above the other buildings on the horizon. We were rad fatties, sure. But we were also rad fatties on a mission.

By the time we reached the Hogsmeade entrance, my mind was already experiencing overload. *There was snow on the roof of every shop! The Hogwarts Express really did "belch" smoke. Where was Ollivander, and was he working today?* There were Butterbeer carts everywhere, and the train conductor didn't sweat even though it was 90 degrees and he was wearing five layers. This place was clearly magical.

Soon after reaching the ride entrance and castle gates, we were greeted by a couple of wizards and witches. Everyone was wearing Hogwarts robes, but no one had any defining colors or badges to show house pride. *That's rude*, I thought. *If you're going to make them wear long black layered clothing outside in the afternoon for minimum wage, at least let them choose so they could wear their house with pride. Also, it would help us know who to avoid.*

I decided that since there was no red and gold or green and black, I would have to guess their houses for them. Having always had an extraordinary skill when it comes to reading people, I was up for the challenge.

The first robed gatekeeper (house indiscernible at the time) directed everyone else toward the right side of the sidewalk but silently pointed to the left when it was our turn to enter. Confused by what at the time seemed like a lucky chance to beat the crowds, we followed the left path until we were stopped by a woman working in the locker room (she was wearing a polo shirt, but her vibe and assistance left no discernible doubt that she was a Gryffindor). I'm sure the "This is either too good to be true or we just got fucked over" look on both of our faces was apparent, because she asked if we were walking on the left side because we wanted to just view the castle or if we actually wanted to ride. "We're definitely here for the ride." She nodded and gestured back toward the right side. "People on the left side don't want to ride; you better head over to this side," she explained.

I pressed my finger to the sensor to unlock a locker. "I think we just got fat clocked by the wizard at the entrance!" Bevin grinned as she lifted her purse to the top locker. It dawned on me that the robed gatekeeper's quick body scan and assumption that we weren't interested in the ride was based purely on the size of our bodies. It was now also apparent to me that while undetectable at the time, he was certainly a Slytherin. That, or really bad at his job.

As we proceeded, my nervousness mounted. Maybe my body just wasn't deserving of the enchanting castle we were about to enter. This was a feeling that I was unfamiliar with, a specific anxiousness that until this point I had somehow managed to escape because of the unmerited comfort I was afforded as a fat person who could still purchase clothing from most plus-size retailers. I hadn't yet been banished to the hinterlands of "extended plus" clothing, only available in shapeless cuts and nondescript knits in the back corners of the internet. I had become accustomed to certain luxuries even while remaining visibly fat in a world designed for thin people.

We passed the room full of chattering portraits, and the frame with the Fat Lady,[6] and paused for a moment in front of the Sorting Hat, which spouted advice from its perfectly crumpled scowl.

After passing Dumbledore's office, a young, curly-haired wizard stopped us (Hufflepuff *definitely*) and requested that I try their sample seat before getting into the final line.

"Nah, I'm good!" My response made him visibly uncomfortable. "I mean, the chair I want to test is the one I'm going to actually be in. I don't want to turn back yet, do I?" He mumbled something that sounded like an agreement. I asked if he had a recommendation for which seat would be the biggest on the ride, and some of the discomfort left his face as he was finally able to help. "The third one from the left" he said. "That's the big one."

Retaining some optimism simply from being *inside* Hogwarts, we practically skipped toward the official ride's giant moving sidewalk. A continuous and seemingly infinite loop of black-belt material, it

----

6. Who, if in line, also might face the possibility of not fitting on the ride, along with Hagrid, Madame Maxime, and certainly "piggish" assholes like Vernon or Dudley; this irony wasn't lost on me.

delivered quickly moving seats, and the employees just as quickly directed guests to their chairs. "I NEED A FAT PERSON THIRD SEAT," I yelled over the deafening noise of the moving ride to the witch who was seating us. I have no idea what house she was from, as by then my small bundle of nerves had grown into a full ball and I was just focused on making this ride work.

She motioned us to the car that had just arrived, and after it emptied I hopped into the third seat, noticing that it was a bit taller than the other three. Bevin sat beside me in a slightly smaller seat two (*bold decision!*), and we pulled our plastic harnesses over our shoulders. I heard Bevin's click loudly into place as I wrapped my arms around mine and pulled down.

It hit my thighs and stopped. No click.

Nothing.

A tiny witch bounced over to us to check our safety status and said, "Ma'am, this is only tightened to a number one, and it has to be pulled down to a three to ride." I asked her if perhaps *she* could push it down any further since I was trapped in a three-sided plastic box. "I can't," she shook her head.

We were quickly ushered off of the moving walkway and through a dungeon (yep, a fucking dungeon), following an obviously uncomfortable wizard who promised that we would be able to find a solution for this seating issue. The solution turned out to be a trip back to the hapless Hufflepuff whose request to sit in a trial seat I had denied. Neither of us were thrilled to meet again, but my face was as flushed with determination as his ears were pink from having a job where causing potential humiliation was simply part of his post.

I hopped into the three-sided plastic tester seat like a good tourist this time, and he attempted to click the trial harness. Again, it stopped at my thighs. So I slammed it down harder. Same outcome. I couldn't have been the first person to have failed the test, but he still seemed at a loss for how to address the situation. "I'm sorry, ma'am," he stammered, "but I don't think this ride is going to work."

"Well, can you push harder?" I asked, thinking of the completely unhelpful (and solution-promising liar of an) employee on the moving walkway who in hindsight probably deserved forgiveness because, after all, she was so small she likely couldn't have helped if she wanted to.

"I can't."

"Jesus Christ." I looked Bevin directly in the eyes. *"I'm going to need you to squish me, girl."* I didn't have to ask twice; she knew what needed to be done. She strode up to the seat and, with all of the effort she could, slammed down the plastic harness. Nothing.

"JUMP!" I yelled as a crowd started to gather to watch a tattooed fat girl getting smashed by another fat glitter-covered blonde.

As commanded, Bevin grabbed the bottom piece and, using every ounce of her body weight, jumped up and came down as hard as possible, leaning on it and pushing it as far as it would go. Which was still . . . the top of my thighs.

There was no other solution to be tried. No other dungeon to be escorted through. I had my answer. JES BAKER DOES NOT FIT INTO HARRY POTTER AND THE FORBIDDEN JOURNEY.

And there you have it. I was officially a theme-park reject, a member of the Too Fat to Fly on a Broomstick club. I had been through the initiation, one where they pointed you out of the castle and practically handed you a Pottermore-emblazoned bag full of body shame to take with you as a consolation prize.

We walked out, making cheerful (and purposefully distracting) conversation about what other shops we were going to visit as if we hadn't just performed an amazing Fat Girl Circus act in front of dozens of other Harry Potter lovers.

I slowly processed the event as we passed Ollivanders wand shop. "Bevin, what size do you wear, and how much do you weigh?"

She nonchalantly answered, "I usually wear a size 20/22 and weigh 297." I stopped walking.

"*Me too!*" I exclaimed, completely stunned. Me too as in, I wear the same size and weigh exactly that amount. Her seat clicked effortlessly. I had a person weighing almost three hundred pounds attempting to force my restraint down by jumping astoundingly high in the air and I couldn't even come close to the safety requirements.

We stopped at a bench to record a video about our findings (something that could easily serve as an audition tape for a future *Fat Oprah* show) and document how two fat bodies with the exact amount of fat-looking poundage could both fit easily and also *not at all* into the same ride. Fat bodies are shaped differently. Standardized sizing isn't a thing. Universal simply didn't make seats for stockier fats.

This wasn't my weight's fault, after all, but rather a decision made by a company that carelessly excluded customers with diverse body types. My Gryffindor pride was bruised with this realization, but not broken.

We then stepped into the Three Broomsticks, chatted with three magnificent Slytherins, and ordered a couple Butterbeers. That is not a sentence I ever thought I would get to type.

While we sat next to a fireplace with an enormous cauldron, I had my phone in hand, ready to document whatever magic was left in our trip. And as I swiped through my apps, I found that I didn't have the urge to google weight-loss methods again. Not this time. It became clear to me that fatness wasn't the actual problem. Bevin had fit into the ride effortlessly, while I couldn't get the goddamn plastic harness anywhere near the bottom half of the belt. This overturned the blame I had placed on my weight and made my searching for drastic surgery opportunities seem like a misplaced answer to an unconnected problem.

Throwing away my learned lessons about how "Fat People Don't Deserve Shit," we left the Three Broomsticks and headed to the front to ask for a refund. We were offered not only a kind apology and full refund, but also the option to spend the rest of the day at the park "on the house."

We politely declined, walked out the doors, and made the best decision of the day: *"Who wants to go shop at Lush?!?!"*

....

My desperation-fueled search for lap-band surgery solutions while in the car waiting for Andy was not the first time I've taken to the internet to do this sort of frenzied fat-reductive research. Multiple times in my life, I've read about magical fat-removal procedures—from the "safer" alternatives to the most drastic. Any intentions to follow through with these types of surgeries have obviously not been executed, but after this particular parking lot theme park–induced fat-based freak-out, the rumination around a faux surgical solution stayed with me. Longer than I expected.

I often wonder if other fat people dedicated to body liberation also think about getting weight-loss surgery. It's seemingly impossible to find this out by looking at most body-image spaces on the internet, as it's a topic that is vehemently rejected in most fat spaces, which I understand. But, even still, I couldn't help but think that I am not alone in occasionally wondering what my life would be like if I lived in a drastically smaller body and if weight-loss surgery were the way to get me there.

Phone calls and Skype sessions with those I find to be brilliant figures in this movement have revealed to me that *so many* fat people struggle with this internal battle between what is deemed "good" and "evil." Of course we all do. How could we not?

While cognizant that the social consequences of fatness are the driving force behind feeling the need to shrink our bodies, we still manage to conflate that outside pressure with what feels like a "natural" dissatisfaction with fatness. Even when we know that our bodies aren't wrong and that society is steeped in unfair bias, it doesn't change the harassment fat people face every day. It doesn't change the judgment that is passed when we apply for job interviews or the leers from students and teachers in academia who feel as if we're not smart enough to attend classes. There are roadblocks everywhere we turn, and when offered a "way out," sometimes we all wonder what could be.

Everyone I've broached this topic with agreed that thinness would make life easier. And almost all of us admitted *not only* to contemplating drastic measures like weight-loss surgery, *but also* to feeling barricaded from ever speaking about these treacherous words in public.

We know, undoubtedly, that if these secret wishes were spoken aloud within our communities, we would become the next Ashley Tipton. The next Gabourey Sidibe. The next Rosie Mercado.[7] The next alleged failure who couldn't hack it and succumbed to the fat-hating world we all continuously fight against. There is a shame in these spaces that comes when you don't like your body, and it almost seems as if the less we talk about it, the easier it becomes to never speak of it again.

A friend shared the story of one of her close friends, a fellow political and radical fatty who had undergone weight-loss surgery but was so terrified of the scathing responses she was sure she would receive that she told no one. Not one person in her community.

....

7. I'm unable to type this list without recognizing that these visible individuals who have undergone weight-loss surgery (and were consequently punished by online humiliation as penance for buying into surgically-based diet culture) are *all* women of color. This brings up so many questions: why weren't Rosie O'Donnell or Roseanne Barr the subject of as many scathing articles? Do women of color feel the pressure to participate in weight-loss surgery more than white women? And how many of the livid responses that come from the fat community are racist expectations for women of color to put up with the impossible? What happens when we mix racism, sexism, and sizeism, both in fat communities and beyond? We need to be asking these questions in this conversation too.

She died in her house from surgical complications soon after, without anyone knowing. Her body wasn't found until three days later.

This is what happens when we don't have the scary conversations about the realities of being fat. That it's hard. That we falter. That we think the "unthinkable." That sometimes it becomes too much. That sometimes we know others will brand us a failure for these things and so we purse our lips together and never share the truth. This is not only an issue when it comes to communication failure but around life and death as well.

I'd like to think that conversations about both liberation and ir-resolution can exist simultaneously and imperfectly. I'd like to think we can become capable of acknowledging multiple sides of a situation. Neither of these come easily.

As advocates, activists, and marginalized folx, we are all balancing two worthy, diverging goals: being on the front lines of battling the status quo while attempting to heal ourselves. So, our reactions and responses to any idea that isn't entirely against the status-quo are often intense and visceral, and rightfully so. I believe that having full and difficult conversations is necessary, but when we have all worked so hard to reject a culture that is still imposed on us every day, making room for potentially harmful thoughts from others becomes difficult, maybe even impossible; I don't know, exactly. I certainly have days when I fail in this department.

But if even determined body activists are terrified to tell their truth when they have the platform and ability to share it, who can? And by suggesting that we have these conversations about this, I am leading us into a quagmire of questions.

How much are we allowed to change our bodies while still being body positive? Does that amount of change decrease if we call ourselves part of the fat acceptance movement? Does the community get to vote you out if you go over a line? Where is the line? Does a group of people on a social media platform count as a community?

How many people need to be a part of this group for it to be considered legit? If it's a secret group, does that make it even more official? Is there a goddamn body-image deity I can pray to and ask all of these questions? A body-image president, maybe, whom I can write a letter to? Does someone want to hand me a fortune cookie with a bland message in it that I can twist to answer this long-ass list of ethical dilemmas? Where do we have full conversations? Did someone already tweet a survey about where these lines are and I missed it? Why is Twitter so hard for me to understand when even Justin Bieber can use it? Where do we challenge the almighty doctors, who are just as biased as the rest of the world? Where do we decide what is best for both our mental and physical health? What do we use as mile markers for ourselves, and what lines do we allow those we inadvertently put our trust in to cross? Are you allowed to talk about Flat Tummy Tea and how it helps bloating when some use it for weight loss?[8] Are you allowed to focus on pounds when your plantar fasciitis demands it? How many times can you fail to reach body neutrality before you're not a representative of body positivity or fat acceptance? Whose approval matters and whose doesn't? How many times can you contemplate lap-band surgery and not be labeled a weakened hypocrite? How many times can you change your body and still be true to yourself and considered body positive enough for everyone else?

Or, are we all just out there making due with our lot in life while trying to deal with whatever body we were born into in order to mentally survive without getting physically trampled?

Damn, *do I have questions.*

....

8. Nah, probably not, but that's just me, and I'm definitely not a sanctioned judge or jury here.

Just in case you're now skimming this chapter to find out all of the answers, I'll tell you right now *that I honestly don't have them.* If anything, I might be more confused by this than you are.

I alter my body in many ways, for so many reasons.

I am covered in tattoos. I think I stopped counting at twenty, as they all started to blend and include a three-quarter sleeve I never finished. This is a way in which I have drastically altered my body. It's radical in some circles, blasé in others, but I have been refused jobs because of it. Are tattoos an acceptable alteration when it comes to body liberation?

I started laser hair removal[9] on my face after years of dealing with the bearded side effects of PCOS. I know people who grow and love the beard, people who shave twice a day, people who wax it often, and people who use those terrifying coiled-spring contraptions that I could never figure out how to use painlessly to get rid of the same kind of facial hair. Are some of these people more "body positive" than I am? Are we all supposed to let it grow in order to embrace our body the way it is? Is a temporary "fix" okay because that means we can revert back to our naturally hairy selves when we realize that we're buying into Beauty Myth Bullshit? Am I a failure because I've chosen a permanent removal process? Does it matter that I made this decision only after finding peace with my facial hair and acknowledging my unwavering worth regardless of how much hair I have or don't have on my face?[10]

....

9. Basically a fifteen-minute nap in a padded doctor's chair where you wear metal tanning goggles while they run a light over your face, and after feeling like you just got snapped with eighty microscopic rubber bands, you leave smelling like burnt hair.

10. Additionally, what about the links between trans liberation and body liberation? What about people who've never had the chance to "accept" their body? If there is a consensus that we're all supposed to love our bodies, is gender-confirming care part of body liberation? Or does all of this come down to the same thing: personal consent?

I take medication for chronic depression and complex PTSD. These on their own cause weight gain (a body change), and additionally they save my life. Within the last year, I also started temporarily taking a drug called Vyvanse, which is often prescribed for ADHD but can additionally help with binge-eating disorder. The suggestion for this prescription came when I shared with my psychiatrist how I often eat late at night to the point of feeling sick in order to ward off depression and sedate my body so I can survive another day. I explained that this binging was mentally needed for comfort, so it was a normal part of my night routine. I often felt out of control with these compulsory actions because they would leave me feeling physically ill as I crawled into bed. He offered this suppressant that was used to treat binge-eating disorder as a solution, and my immediate reaction was to recoil in horror.

"Like, a diet pill?" I whispered, feeling the terror of something like this entering into my life again. He assured me that it wasn't.

I battled with myself for months about the addition of Vyvanse, even though it was a temporary solution.

I couldn't discern where Vyvanse fell on the scale from "helping my brain chemistry" to "making me an unforgivable traitor." This was a decision that could potentially change what feels like my identity—a person who believes in fat liberation. Was this identity worth compromising just so I could feel better? Was assisting my brain more important than the relationships I had formed in body-positive spaces?

I started with what I knew: I gratefully take medication for a chemically imbalanced brain that is prone to depression, and I couldn't be more of an advocate for this. That was 100 percent okay in my book. Weight-loss surgery? Not an option. Surgery is an external force created to make me less fat, something I refuse to buy into. *However*, I argued with myself, what "I knew" starting to become fuzzy, *Vyvanse is also an external force. But it wasn't created for weight loss*, I came back at myself with this fact. This medication's simple link to eating made it nearly impossible for me to untangle its usefulness from my complex history with fatness.

This back-and-forth continued for what felt like forever. I decided, hesitantly, to try it for a short while to see how it made me feel. I was at liberty to stop taking it whenever I chose. There was no rubber band that refused to let me eat or permanent surgery involved; I still had complete control over my body and brain chemistry. I was terrified but willing to try.

A few weeks after I started taking The Pill That Must Not Be Named, I found myself sitting cross-legged on the floor of the Dallas airport typing on my computer while waiting for my next connection, completely unaware of the TGI Friday's across from me. It was then that I first realized that something was different. While I felt no "physical" effects, there was a subtle mental shift that became more and more obvious as I realized what I was *not* doing in an airport for the first time in maybe, ever.

Up until that hour or so spent in the Dallas Delta terminal, my previous layovers (we're talking numbers in the seventies) were centered around my primary concern: to locate the nearest place to find food. After flying so often, I quickly became a living, breathing airport map of available restaurants no matter the city I had landed in. After all, when your traveling accommodations are made by an outside party for work (like most of mine are, hashtag blessed), you're often left with no idea of what sort of sustenance will be available when you hop off the plane. It's also valid to wonder if any food will be available at all.[11] This, in addition to my fucked-up history with

....

11. Shout out to the college in a city made of snowy mountains that didn't have Lyft or Uber and placed me in a hotel miles away from the nearest restaurant (which technically didn't matter because sidewalks didn't exist and the roads were covered in several inches of ice) where I didn't get cell-phone reception and couldn't find a single place that delivered. It's a damn good thing I like peanut paste sandwiched between cheddar-flavored crackers from a vending machine. A *damn* good thing.

food scarcity, means knowing where the nearest Potbelly is has become one of my most honed talents. When you grow up wondering if there will be enough food in the fridge to feed the family, this panic feels very real.

But I wasn't feeling any shitty-half-the-size-of-what-you'd-get-at-a-regular-restaurant-for-twice-the-cost anxiety that day. I wasn't rushing to the hostess desk and requesting the first seat they had available. I wasn't seeing what was closer or which line was shortest. I was working on a presentation, my mind focused on something else rather than the food I usually needed to remain calm.

This little blue-and-white pill was releasing me from internal panic and compulsion. And while I still felt unable to parse out how my brain, its relationship with eating disorders, and my physical fatness all fit together, I could feel some strange semblance of mental balance. A balance that felt similar to the evenness that comes when I take Xanax when having panic attacks. Or the Prozac that I take for chronic depression. Or the Lamictal that evens out my moods. Those last three medications bring my mind from a place of instability to a place of balance that has allowed me to live my best life.

And yet Vyvanse, even though it was being used in the exact same way, still causes me internal struggle. Is taking this medication a moral sin? Was I supposed to feel sick every night instead of succumbing to this blue-and-white pill? Should I be "stronger" mentally and push through the trauma? Was it okay to take as long as I was working with a non-diet dietician, who was helping me heal the actual underlying problems?

I shave my legs. I wear lipstick. I wax my eyebrows. I'm on a birth control that I know makes me gain weight and I choose to let it alter my body anyway. These are small, simple things, but I still wonder.

I find myself without any answers when it comes to changing my body. I run through all the options and ask myself where the cutoff is. How much do I have to *not* conform in order to still be "body positive?" Where exactly is the *This Is Assimilation!* line, and have I crossed it?

The weight-loss conversation is inherently complicated and weighty (bad pun—I'm sorry). Just like humans want the quickest and simplest way to lose weight, we also want hard-and-fast directions as to how to rid ourselves of body shame and oppression. But the gray is where we must sit if we want to have a full conversation. And there is no landing pad in the gray area, only uncertainty. Uncertainty when you're looking for freedom doesn't feel like a solution at all.

I see why weight loss and the discussion around it can become controversial. We need a place where we can find solace from the oppression that surrounds us everywhere else. We need to have support for the days where the "simple" act of living feels impossible. We need people who get it. We need a community that will give the middle finger to everything that tries to harm us.

The question then becomes, how do we integrate these hard feelings that are triggering, uncertain, and dangerous into our conversations so that no one is found dead and alone because they didn't feel safe sharing their body decisions with a group that believed it was their right to have a say in those decisions? How do we safely say it all?

Other than understanding that we all need to become each other's healing partners, I don't know.

As a person who wants to empower others and *not* add more restrictions, I think the only possible route is to let each person make decisions about their own body without external judgment or shame. Each body belongs to its inhabitant (not to the world at large or to the fat community) and its inhabitant only. Complete body autonomy. Not only for fat bodies, but all bodies—every single fucking one. To demand anything else seems a slippery slope I can't see the end of.

In an ideal world, we would not take others' decisions personally. We wouldn't need to, because we wouldn't feel such a scarcity of love and acceptance. We wouldn't cling so tightly to the small handful of fat household names. We wouldn't carry the trauma of living in a society that takes every opportunity to remind fat people that we are less than.

Many disagree with me. Many fierce body advocates say that this is unforgivable. I counter that no one owes the community their entire life and body, that there is no forgiveness needed. Perhaps a person's choice will affect those who appreciate them. Perhaps they will need to accept the consequences of losing trust. I hope we can move further, breaking down stigmas within our own communities and healing those broken places with compassion. Marginalized communities have the power to heal each other; if anyone understands the reality of our situations, it would be us. But this will require an immense amount of work on all of our parts.

For now, I find myself thinking that perhaps there is no wrong or right. There just is.

That is what I'm sticking with.

When we zoom out of our microscopic online communities and look at people like Ashley, we see one person pitted against and forced to battle industry gods—weight-loss and beauty industry gods armed with hundreds of years of gaslighting rhetoric and billions of dollars. It isn't a fair fight.

And yet, when an individual loses this unfair war, we are quick to point directly at them and say *you* have failed. If only you tried harder. If only you had been braver. David beat Goliath with one stone, and you couldn't even handle *this*? The shame and failure lie on you.

And Goliath goes free once again.

But maybe, just maybe, we have it all wrong.

Maybe not all of us have to kill Goliath. It's possible that not everyone has the skill set or slingshot to take down a behemoth with one stone. Maybe just some people have these resources and perhaps only some can fight the way so many of us expect them to. And maybe, just maybe, those who can't have every right to wave their white flag in the valid quest for survival.

....

My personal sadness lies in a different area than most when it comes to a fat person's decision to engage in weight-loss surgery. It is tragic that so many fat people feel such intense pressure to give up the only bodies they've ever had. It's frustrating that a procedure like weight-loss surgery can feel like a direct buy into the capitalism, diet culture, and internalized fatphobia that cornered fat people in the first place.

But on top of all that, there is also the undeniable fact that this sort of assimilation into thinness—or even the attempt at assimilation—will be rewarded tenfold by society. There will be a celebration. Before and after photos. Copious amounts of congratulations. The chance to climb a ladder toward success that fatter bodies aren't allowed to even step on.

The sad part for me is not that someone chose to have surgery in order to survive this sizest world; my sorrow is deeply entrenched in the fact that *it works so well.*

Perhaps in the end, the answer is to acknowledge that each and every person's journey is flexible, malleable, and ever changing. And that none of it is right or wrong.

Don't think that I'm coming from a place of "We should all hold hands and sing kumbaya!" That's a place where change doesn't happen and issues are swept under the rug, never to be resolved. But it is our disposability culture that is currently making it impossible to have dialogue around these critical issues that many fat people face. We, for whatever reason, feel the need to separate people into two sections: good and evil; perfect or completely problematic. This is where the conversation erases the middle ground, which is where, as humans, we all live.

I think acknowledging the *and* is the most important part when it comes to fat folks and our discussion of our bodies. It's important that we see both sides. That we respect body autonomy but also grieve other people's decisions. To indict someone for the "moral failure" of surgery not only releases the Goliath-esque industry from taking responsibility for its harmful actions but can also lead to a situation where we, as members of the fat community, start to feel as if others owe us their body. Which, when we think about it, is the exact same thing we are fighting against as we pursue body liberation from societal standards.

I sincerely want every person to have permission to sit with whatever feelings arise when they watch prominent figures change their body, allowing themselves to process that grief, betrayal, and existential sorrow. We must be allowed to feel to their fullest extent whatever emotions arise; it's a healing necessity. I also believe that having safe spaces where we can find reprieve from a fatphobic culture and its outcomes is needed. It is my hope that we can work on healing together so that when someone chooses something that triggers us, we are able to let them own their own journey as we remain steadfast in ours; that we figure out how to not dispense of an entire, multifaceted person because we feel they have made a mistake. I realize that I'm dreaming of a complicated world. It sounds like pie-in-the-sky thinking, but I still hope to God that we end up there. Because, just maybe, we can create an even better world for those struggling with feelings they are currently too afraid to voice. Maybe then we could navigate the nuances that would allow us to both offer support and work toward healing ourselves. Perhaps the answer lies in an area that we haven't been able to explore just yet.

I'm crossing my fingers that we reach this state of community support and conversation, not only because implementing this concept has the potential to allow radical and personal liberation, but also because it would mean that Paula would probably text me less in the early hours of the morning.

And Lord *knows* I need my sleep.

CHAPTER 17

The Pros and Cons of Being Fat

PRO: Better airplane seats because of "unmentionable" problems.

TECHNOLOGY HAS IN the last ten years changed the way I travel in more positive ways than I can count. While I still panic while packing the night before, the airport process has become almost futuristic compared to the trips I took a decade ago. I now check in before I arrive on my handheld computer, skip the luggage check (the longest line in the airport aside from the one at Starbucks), and seamlessly move through security, which then gives me time to check the airline's app to study the seating arrangements before I board. I then arm myself with information regarding what seats are full and what seats are blessedly empty before walking myself down that tight aisle where everyone is secretly hoping I am not their seatmate. That part is unfortunately exactly the same as it was ten years ago. But having those newfangled pre-boarding options before you have to walk down the narrow cabin carpet? It's amazingly convenient, almost like a dream within a nightmare, and fuck if I know how this is even possible.

Occasionally you can move and get better seats on an airplane if there are two empty ones side by side by politely flagging down a flight attendant and asking if you might be able to move to those chairs, casually slipping in that it's *"because of my size."*

"Because of my size" is the adult version of the high school excuse to leave class because of "lady problems." People get awkward, embarrassed, and will usually say "yes" as quickly as possible just so everyone can move on and they can pretend that they didn't just obviously look me up and down before agreeing.

Nothing makes some passengers angrier than a fat person's not being actively punished or publicly dehumanized for daring to get on a plane. In fact, if those fatphobic travelers were to read this super tip for plus-size flyers, I wouldn't be surprised if they had a heart attack[1] induced purely from rage over the fact that we not only are refusing to be humiliated for flying but also are finding a way to use the airline system so that it works to our advantage.

My response? Fuck 'em.

You paid for a seat, they paid for a seat. That obnoxious drunk asshole paid for a seat, and the mother with a screaming child paid for a seat. The lady vomiting in the paper bag paid for a seat, and that young guy blaring YouTube videos on his phone because he doesn't like headphones paid for a seat. Planes are not meant to feel like an all-inclusive resort (though if I had a million dollars I'd totally try one of those sleeper planes). It's simply a demoralizing but functional way to shuttle humans across the world, and it's going to be stressful and uncomfortable for everyone because that's just how flying is.

....

1. Those aren't just reserved for the obesity crisis, you know.

Should you ever have the opportunity to fly, do yourself a favor and advocate for yourself.[2] There is no reason for self-flagellation when you walk down a plane aisle. You deserve to feel comfortable and be treated like a human just like every other passenger. Something else to keep in mind? If anything, moving to a seat with more room benefits everyone.

CON: Airplane bathrooms.

While there are definitely ways to make flying more comfortable when you have a larger body, there is one aspect that will forever be the bane of a fat flyer's existence: the godforsaken airplane restroom.

Alternative name #1: A literal tiny water *closet*

Alternative name #2: A contained area barely big enough to fit two suitcases

Alternative name #3: Hell

One thing that is rarely admitted is that when you're fat, you need a little more wiggle room to finish your bathroom business. It's nothing more than a logistical space issue. When trying to wipe your ass without substantial room to move your body into an efficient position, you'll likely find yourself attempting unrealistic yoga positions that you doubt are taught in any class. And while there was a time when yoga was a daily part of my life, I never learned the modified "Leg Over Shoulder" pose needed to successfully accomplish what many people can (I assume) effortlessly do when they are not my size.

Thank you, God, for safety rails and their unwavering support.

....
2. Things to remember: 1) Don't be afraid to ask for a seat-belt extender; 2) You don't need to apologize for existing; and 3) Make sure to join the Facebook group "Flying While Fat" for all the insider tips!

Listen up, Delta. I want a blue ribbon or 60,000 flyer miles for having to perform this magician-worthy feat. Though, I suppose I would be happy with a first-class seat and vodka tonic.

I sometimes wonder how extra tall, larger, and/or physically disabled people manage this as well. I have often heard from close fat friends that they refrain from eating up to twenty-four hours before flying so this basic necessity isn't an obstacle. It's almost like they're preparing for a colonoscopy, only it's something far worse. Its bigotry and capitalism combined, and it makes a basic human need impossible for many humans. I am still unable to wrap my mind around how unbelievably fucked this is.

Using an airplane bathroom while fat and/or tall/disabled should be an award-winning act that is congratulated with a ribbon after you slide the lock back from Occupied to Vacant and emerge victoriously into a cabin full of seats that weren't designed with you in mind.

And those who can't even fit in the bathroom and are denied a basic and universal need? They deserve free tickets. Or better yet, a plane built to accommodate all bodies. How's that for a highfalutin idea?

PRO: This hella sexy ass.

Enough said.

CON: Birth control nurses think they're your therapist.

Ever since I started working in the food industry, was paid in tips, and was denied health insurance, I've used the Pima County Health Clinic to receive my birth control. In theory it sounds like a simple excursion, but in reality, it turns into a premeditated obstacle course if you have any interest in getting in and out in under five hours. You learn to show up a half hour before they open and take your place in line outside the door, resentfully standing behind the people who were smarter than you and got there forty-five minutes early. When the doors open, you rush Black Friday style to the receptionist's desk to make sure that you're seen as soon as possible—I may have insinuated once that seeing a nurse before the next time I had sex would be preferable.

I've managed to master this public contraception game over the years, though, and it's continued to work, becoming a sterile-smelling luxury that I appreciate because the alternative option of visiting a primary care physician's office as a fat person (which can be more tortuous than reading any Yahoo comment section because fatphobia lives everywhere—even in clinical spaces we're told to trust) is a miserable thing to commit to. And so, I perform this routine every three months. At least I know what to expect when I get there: a long wait, cranky nurses, a depo shot, and an occasionally odd comment about my weight.

The Pima County Health Clinic is nothing if not consistent.

After your name is called, you walk into a tiny room and sit down with a nurse, who asks if any of your medication has changed, the last time you had your period, and if you would stand on the scale. Each time, I say, "No, they haven't in five years, it's spotty and unpredictable, and I would rather not."

Seven times out of ten they will semi-politely challenge my refusal to be weighed,[3] but when I ask why they need a number when I was *just* there three months ago, the surprise isn't hidden when they reply, "Well, to see if you're gaining weight while on the Depo shot."

"Oh, I definitely do," is always my answer. Hesitant to accept this and flustered by this dismissive fat girl who of *all people* should be hypervigilant about stepping on the scale, they somehow manage to

---

3. Little known fact: You are absolutely permitted to refuse to step on a scale at any clinical office. Your body, your rules.

carry on and ask which thigh I prefer to be poked in. Sixty seconds later, I'm injected and more than ready to leave.

Occasionally, though, during this simple procedure I am faced with questions that are inappropriate for any person whose job it is to stick you with an anti-baby needle to ask. More often than not they are manageable, but sometimes? Sometimes they leave me speechless.

I was caught off-guard one morning by a quiz I wasn't prepared for. I methodically answered their routine question: "No, they haven't in five years; it's spotty and unpredictable; and I would rather not."

As the nurse entered this information into the database, she swiveled away from the computer toward me and casually asked, "So, what's your comfort food?"

It was a nurse I hadn't met before, and at that moment I, for the first time in years, was sure that I preferred the abrasively cranky nurse I usually dreaded because her communication skills had the deftness of verbal sandpaper and you never knew if she hated you personally or just hated her life. While usually gruff to the point of making you squirm in your seat, I did enjoy the appointment where she insisted on showing me how to properly use a condom on a wooden penis. I stifled a laugh at the absurdity of sitting in a small room learning how to pinch the tip of a condom on an oak-made cock from a grouchy woman who reminded me of Roz, the spectacularly cantankerous receptionist from *Monsters, Inc.*

I would have taken a wooden-penis demonstration over this conversation any day.

When I gave the new nurse a blank stare after this bizarre and weirdly inappropriate question, she asked again: "What is your favorite thing to eat for comfort?" Maybe I didn't understand.

Baffled at why my birth-control distributor was asking me this and unsure how to answer, I continued to sit silently.

"Y'know? Comfort food? Mine is ice cream!" she offered this information with a forced smile in a way that showed she thought that discussing something from her secret life would perhaps create a lifetime bond, or at the very least put me at ease.

I gathered all of the patience I could muster and said in my calmest voice, "I'm here to ensure that I don't have a baby, and you want to know, not about my diet, which is my PCP's business, if anything, but what I eat out of compulsion? I feel like these questions are inappropriate and irrelevant to this situation since I'm here for a needle full of hormones and nothing else."

She was caught off-guard. "Oh. Well, I was just wondering about the weight gain." I reminded her that she'd already asked me about this, and she quickly changed the subject and asked what I was doing over the weekend. I can't remember my answer; it was likely something boring about scheduling work meetings and printing out invoices.

Stab, band aid, checkout.

I groaned as half a dozen burn-worthy responses came to me as I unlocked my car.[4] The brilliance always comes when I'm getting behind the steering wheel.

It's probably for the best.

CON: DAMN, do you get trolled.

It has been clear to me for years now that when I die (and I assuredly will, as all humans do) there will be a magnificent online celebration. The number of attendees is hard to estimate, and I doubt that I

....
4. After talking with poet and fellow rad fatty Rachel Wiley about this experience, she offered this blistering gem that I'm keeping in my pocket for my next checkup: "I would've told her that my comfort food is babies, and since that is frowned upon by society, she'd better just inject those hormones and keep my reign of terror at bay."

could dig deep enough on the internet to make an accurate assumption, so I'll just roughly quote: hundreds. It's likely more in the range of thousands, but I don't want to flatter myself.

It's strange to know that complete strangers will find immense joy in dancing on my internet grave, but I'm not alone in this. It's safe to assume that anyone who is visible online shares this reality, but I still struggle to comprehend that this celebration will occur simply because I have the gall to publicly encourage others to pursue self-love and share that, as a fat person, I have worth.

Body currency (the hierarchy of desirable bodies within society and the belief that thinner ones are more valuable) is immediately dismantled when someone who is supposed to exist in shame and remorse for their size (or other qualities deemed unacceptable within our ablest, racist, ageist, etc. society) refuses to apologize for their existence. By proclaiming that all bodies are equal in value, I am crushing the hopes and dreams of all those still invested in the belief that the more conventionally attractive you become the happier you will be.

To assert the notion that you can be happy without becoming smaller takes away their pot of gold at the end of the diet culture rainbow and leaves a lot of them, well, pissed. Enraged. Livid. Even murderous, according to hate threads, apparently. Theoretically, I understand why this anger surges within them. But I still refuse to excuse their behavior. I've had pictures taken from my blog and inserted on a thread where a competition took place to see who could leave the most disgusting comment. I've had my BMI guesstimated, my weight tracked, and my statuses archived to use against me should the occasion arise. My personal blog posts have been taken and spun into horror stories and then passed around as truth. There are dozens of people twisting anything and everything I say into a lie so they can "catch me in the act."

It's also been typed more than once on my pages that if I don't want to be bullied, threatened, or afraid for my safety I should simply lose weight. That the onus lies on me as a fat person to either assimilate or reap the repercussions of an animalistic society without complaint. That so many wholeheartedly believe this still stuns me.

To call these individuals Trolls is to dehumanize them and consequently release them of the responsibility of adhering to the basic tenets of humanity. To call them Haters is to trivialize their actions and normalize their horrific behavior. I often wonder what to call them, and sometimes I just resort to "happy, fulfilled people brimming with compassion and living extraordinarily busy lives" because in this case sometimes the only way to explain this phenomenon is to call it exactly what it isn't.

Many people make the assumption that these individuals are living in the basement of their parents' house, miserably taking breaks from microwaving a Hot Pocket and playing World of Warcraft to fill strangers' comments sections with verbal bile.[5] We don't really know who they are, though. The uncomfortable reality is that people who harass others online are the everyday people who surround us. They're the people we move around in public with who occasionally attack fat people publicly but more often than not find that inflicting pain is more convenient when done from behind the safety of their screens.[6]

We might not be able to identify exactly who they are, but one thing I know is that *happy people don't try to harm happy people.* I know this because (aside from logic) I feel like it's impossible to be

....

5. My college and current self still agree that Hot Pockets are the shit.

6. Though, statistically, "trolling" has become the preferred sport of cis white men, so watch out for those guys. Specifically, in my case, they are often in their thirties, fanatically conservative, and obsessed with that "gym life."

happy for other people when I am miserable. My personal experience with these emotional stumbling blocks continues to serve as a needed reminder that when I become a target for hatred from others, it has everything to do with their reality and nothing to do with mine. I always hold on to this reminder while reading comments underneath my Instagram images, like "I love this National Geographic feature of endangered walruses" or "Just kill yourself."[7]

One of the best decisions I made in my online career was to hire a "social media monitor"—a special someone who combs through my pages and comments and does the deleting and banning for me. This allows me to avoid ingesting any online toxicity aimed my way and, even better, has unexpectedly made it so that those dedicated to serious harassment, apparently realizing that their right to comment on my pages would be immediately revoked, have decided to take their hatred to other forums, where they can discuss without consequence the fact that my arms are so disgusting that they're indiscernible appendages. They've migrated to pages notorious for hate speech, and I've learned to not search for them. This is the unspoken agreement that currently rests between us.

This doesn't save me from safety concerns, however. I've managed to simply solve online threats, for the most part, but this doesn't mean that I'm safe in my day-to-day life. I choose pictures I post carefully so that those who actively try to piece together where I live in order to further harass me are unable to do so. I am hypervigilant while shopping and wary of those in line behind me because of a past experience. I hold my breath when interacting with postal workers and delivery drivers, hoping they don't know who I am so that my address can't be used against me. I have to cautiously open mail without full return addresses. When new neighbors move in, I

....
7. I corrected the spelling and grammar, of course, because they are often too busy to do it themselves. I gotcha covered, guys.

pray they are indifferent to my work or, better yet, have no idea who Jes Baker is. And while I have resolved to live my best life, these are valid precautions I have been forced to take so that the harassment doesn't escalate or turn into something even worse—the targeting of my loved ones.

It is an infuriatingly necessary part of my life, and, to be honest, it's complete bullshit. Unfortunately, I don't see this changing anytime in the near future.

There is a ubiquitous and unofficial rule online that we are not to talk about these sorts of issues. "Don't feed the trolls" is advice others have patronizingly (though well-intentionedly) doled out on countless occasions. The underlying assumption is that if we ignore the attacks, they'll go away. I'm here to say: this is *definitely* not true.

I made the personal decision to not engage a few years in (using the standby of delete, block, and move on), but that was simply a tactic to preserve my own sanity and energy. The less I gave in to their rage, the more bandwidth I had to show up for those who needed the support.

It was only when I read Brittany Gibbons' blog post entitled "Fat Girl Job Clarification" that I felt seen and like I had some solidarity in this quest:

> Here's the thing, folks. . . . It is not my motherfucking job
> to teach you how to be nice to fat people. That is something
> you learn from your parents, peers, or from various social
> cues that direct you toward basic human decency.
>
> It is my job to empower the people you belittle, shame,
> and degrade publicly on a daily basis so they can grow to
> see that the horrible crap you dish out to make yourself
> feel better is just that . . . crap. They are who I break barriers
> down for, they are who I wrote the book for, and they are the
> reason I sat on that stage. My message was for them.

But even after adopting this well-executed intention, the harassment has still admittedly taken an enormous toll on my spirit, my heart, and sometimes—in my most vulnerable moments—my will to live.

Let me be clear: in my ideal world, not everyone would applaud me or approve of my work. I don't need that. The only thing I dream about is a reality where I am left alone to live my life by my rules. Silence and safety would be the ultimate gift.

....

It would be a lie to say that working on the internet for half a decade hasn't changed who I am.

I, slowly and over time, became convinced that ALL people were and are horrible. It wasn't a hard conclusion to reach. I've had the unfortunate chance to see people at their worst. Millions of reactionary comments/emails/conversations have shown me some of humanity's worst, most unabashed colors. I have been handed every shred of proof that I've needed to assume that most humans are incapable of compassion and critical thinking. The expectation of *intentional kindness*? Well, that has always seemed out of the question.

Week after week, I sat on my therapist's couch in tears or full of unshakable rage trying to express the inexpressible. Attempting to explain a reality that most people don't live in or, frustratingly, can't comprehend. I'm not convinced she totally understands the true underbelly of the internet, but thankfully she doesn't need to in order to assist me in conquering this online monster. A year ago, she finally said the words I needed to hear: "Jes, *this is killing you.*" And she was right. I had emotionally reached the point where I had nothing left to give.

So I sent out a social media flare. I asked for a love note or two. And I waited.

PRO: The world will show up if you ask.

Beauty in its truest form showed up. In all its handwritten, sticker-covered, mermaid-patch-filled, glitter-dusted glory.

Gifts, inspiring quotes, love letters, music suggestions, cross-stitched unicorns, drawings from reader's (very talented, by the way) children, pieces of art, Vegemite, calming essential oils, rock candy rings and simple words of support. And they're still coming. I don't know if they realized how much I needed them when they dropped them in the mailbox, but the mail I received reminded me of *everything* wonderful in the world.

I've read many of them. I also have piles saved for later. I often pick a few new ones out each morning before I start my day so that I have a beautiful reminder of why persisting is a good decision.

I expected to feel a few warm flutters. What I *did not* expect was to feel a large part of my heart split wide open and to suddenly have energy back once again. In fact, after the first two weeks of overwhelming love notes (I cried at the post office multiple times), the influx of kindness gave me the emotional room I needed to pack half a dozen care packages for other activists I knew could also use a boost. This mail touched them like it touched me.

The kindness and support will continue to ripple out . . . beyond me, beyond the other activists, beyond all of us. I've been so anti-Woo and universal love for so long, yet somehow this community of people has made it possible to reach the lost parts of me that can now acknowledge how empowering compassion and love can be. They have restored my Woo.

I have more room for hope than I have in years. I have more room to give (and appreciatively receive). Being a fat woman on the internet who openly shares her story can break you. But it can also heal you beyond anything you can imagine.

While the internet is full of trolls, it is *also* full of fatties just like you. At long last, we don't have to be the lone fat kid in a group of skinny folks anymore. The internet offers you the ability to form a community of rad fatties that my teenage self needed more than anything.

The internet is the worst thing that has happened to me. It is also the best thing that has happened to me.

PRO? CON? I'm unsure: polo shirts.

Have you ever seen pictures of your fat girl friends when they were kids? Have you ever noticed that there is always one image of them wearing a polo shirt? Have you noticed in your pictures from growing up that you also were photographed in a polo shirt at some point? Polo shirts. All fat and future fat girls wore them.

CON: Gold-star allies.

You know who I'm talking about. Those "radical" people who are sure they are doing the Lord's precious work and deserve a dozen cookies delivered with a bunch of balloons when they acknowledge your inherent beauty *even though* you're fat. I'm not interested in patronizing compliments in the slightest. Oh, and I'm keeping the cookies and balloons for myself. Sorry, totally not sorry.

PRO: My body is inherently political.

It's a strange experience to know that the sheer fact that you exist and leave the house and sometimes do wild things like have fun in public is an active form of defiance. Breathing is literally resistance. Liking yourself? *Preposterously* radical.

And yet, as a fat person in a society that would prefer that I don't exist, and if I do exist that I don't show up in public where they're forced to see my body, my presence in the world will never be apolitical.

Kim Selling powerfully demanded that this be acknowledged while performing her poem "Fat Bottomed Girls" in 2011:

> *Being fat doesn't make me different.*
> *Fuck, I look like America.*
> *But loving that I'm fat*
> *makes me a Pillsbury rebellion.*
> *I hold protests in my mouth every time I eat in public.*
> *Picket signs wallpaper my willing body*
> *when I dance naked in my apartment.*
> *Riots Not Diets is tattooed across my chest.*
> *And I live for the moment when I shock you into silence.*
> *Because being me is fucking political.*
> *And you never voted for this shit.*

I take up a lot of space. Not just physical space but also energetic space. My confident walk challenges strangers' preconceptions and borrows their mental paradigm.[8] My clothing takes up visual space, demanding to be seen.

When I walk through a crowd, people move. They stare. They question. They are forced to acknowledge me when so often their preferred life goal for fat people is that we become invisible.

There is power in taking up space. There is power in challenging social norms. There is power in being fat and daring to exist.

Every day I live my life, I'm winning.

....
8. It also leads to really awkward situations where Target customers assume that just because I walk like I belong in a public space that I work there, even though I've never worn a red shirt with khakis in my life. Perhaps even more embarrassing is the fact that I'm usually able to direct them to the exact spot they're looking for. Friends even text me with questions because having me direct them to the eye drops is faster than finding an actual sales associate.

CHAPTER 18

American Billboard

THERESA WAS THE kind of friend that every irresponsible, broke, and poor-decision making twenty-two-year-old dreams of. She was outgoing and approachable, and effortlessly made friends at every bar she visited with her brilliant smile. She believed that bean, tomato, and Tabasco burritos were a hangover cure (for the record: they still are). She was charmingly freckled, endlessly positive on the surface, and dressed in a way that could only be described as Sexy Tomboy Babe Who Was Always Ready to Go on a Hike but Only in a Sophisticated Placed Like the Alps. And perhaps her most beguiling characteristic was that she had a car.

She was perfect.

For the first few years of my budding (read: drunken) adulthood, she was the best friend I could ask for. Curly red hair, a body frame reminiscent of a curvy Twiggy, the same Target addiction I had, and willing to let me sleep in her bathtub if I drank too many Long Islands . . . with her by my side, I felt like we could go anywhere and do anything. And we sure as hell did.

We spent all of our nonworking hours together, chatting up the seventy-year-old accordion player at a dive bar, taking photos of the sunset on the edge of town, driving to middle-of-nowhere Arizona and jumping out of planes, drinking High Life in my kitchen while talking about very important things like Noam Chomsky, indie music "no one else knew about," and what outfit would best fit our full-scale mannequin named "Champ." For a bit, we lived together in a house with several other full-life livers (okay, party throwers), and we continued our shenanigans even after she moved into a different house. It was one of those friendships where you forget how you met, how long you lived together and where, and all of the unimportant things that are irrelevant when you spend every day together for years.

It wasn't just the burritos and friendship that drew me to her new house, though. She was also a couch-surfing aficionado. For those of you who are unfamiliar with this once-popular website that has become easily forgettable ever since the Airbnb boom, it was a community of people across the world who would offer up their couches (or spare bedrooms) to travelers for the exact fee of zero dollars.

Want to host couch crashers from another city? Well, then you also got to crash for free wherever you wanted. It was a little like our now-coveted Airbnb options, except it was significantly cheaper, didn't cause rent prices to skyrocket because of people buying city blocks to list, and allowed you to get to know the city from the local host's view. These bonuses, though, came with the ever-looming danger that you knew *nothing* about the person in whose living room you were crashing.

Theresa, being the couch-surfing enthusiast she was, could be counted on to regularly have a new person (or five) from a different country enjoying the space to stash their luggage in her living room while we sat on the front porch smoking, drinking, and listening to said foreign travelers explain why every other country was better than America. Regardless of what they were trying to say, that was always my takeaway.

I could listen to someone talk about anything in a German accent all day long. British too. French also. You get the idea.

It didn't take long for me to start obsessing about a trip to Europe.

When you have a friend who loves to host couch surfers, spends summers in Europe, and brings back a clearly asshole of a boyfriend from Germany after a few months of living in Stuttgart (she refused to admit the truth about his personality but regularly hacked into his email to see if he was cheating), if you wait long enough . . . the opportunity to travel to Europe is bound to come up.

And it did.

After convincing my boss to trust me with an advance, I purchased my ticket, and Theresa generously volunteered to pay for everything else (praying to the Broke Barista Gods works). We immediately set off for London and then Italy. Well, almost. There was a massive volcano eruption and every flight was grounded for a month. After they were flying again, we finally hopped on that twelve-hour flight—unhindered, young, and with unearned ease.

During the George Bush Jr. era, Theresa had believed that traveling abroad was easier if people didn't know that you were American. She would often assume Canadian characteristics and accents when meeting strangers in order to escape the ambush of hatred that often followed the statement "I'm from the U.S.," a direct result of how the world felt about the Bush administration. By the time our trip rolled around, however, this wasn't as much of a concern since we were optimistically traveling from "Yes, We Can" Obama country. But even still, citizenship aside, I was well aware that no matter where I traveled, my body would travel with me.

I could perfect a Canadian accent and know inconsequential facts about Calgary, but my body would never fail to give my home country away. I don't know if I could ever pass as anything other than American, no matter how many times I worked "eh" into a sentence.

Theresa might be able to pass as a waifish, cheerful, curly-haired Canadian, but I would never have that luxury.

....

And it all comes down to my body. My tattooed body, sure. But even more so, my fat body.

I had an obsessive love-hate relationship with the crude, clown-hating, American-trash-talking, food-obsessed, tattooed Anthony Bourdain. I adored swooning over his self-deprecating humor and made a sport out of yelling at the screen when he hypocritically scorned the idea of being a tourist while being one of the most active tourists on television. He was the best and the worst. He was internationally traveling magic with an astounding amount of charming assholery on the side.

I loved him unequivocally for years. Until I didn't.

During an episode of *The Layover* filmed in Rome, he sat at an outdoor café and read from the travel guidebook that he contemptuously but often consulted.

He read out loud: "Most Italian employees go on vacation in August. If you come at that time of year you'll find an almost empty city." He paused to scoff. "Well, that's not true. It will be *clogged* with tourists."

His disdainful reading continued: "If you love watching the glamorous Romans, it's better to visit Rome in the late spring or fall." Unable to take the book seriously any longer, he instead turned his head to glare at a passerby. "On the other hand, if, like me, you just love watching ugly tourists waddle past, slowly frying in the mid-summer sun, y'know, July is fine."

And thus ended our torrid love affair he knew nothing about. I am apparently incapable of loving a fatphobic asshat no matter how hilariously sarcastic they are.

But the sadness over the ending of a secret, decade-long relationship wasn't the most painful part. The true knife that pierced my heart was hearing my biggest fear about traveling while fat spoken out loud. Though slightly veiled, the sentiment was clear: fat, and consequently ugly, tourists (likely from America) were a sickening scourge to every country they visited.

I heard the message loud and clear. It's something I'd privately suspected but until then had never heard vocalized. It made it more real than ever before.

I know that at first glance, to some, I *am* America. To many, I'm everything that's repulsive about America. I am gluttony. I am crass. I am covered in tattoos and usually dress in revealing or tight-fitting clothing. In essence, I am showcasing how unnecessarily excessive and vulgar our country is simply by existing.

I am also Jes Baker. I am a compassionate human with strong feelings about living-room rugs; I believe cats are superior pets, will make you cry after you lose seven hands of Gin Rummy to me, and prefer my coffee in the form of espresso shots.

But when I travel, my complexities as a human are compressed into one thing: I become The United States of Holy Shit.

But I traveled anyway. Unable to ignore my magnetic attraction to London, which I was sure was like New York City, just with crumpets and tea instead of bagels and coffee, I believed that it would give every notable city in my country a run for its money. And honestly, I was right.

Theresa and I hopped off the plane, and I was immediately greeted with everything I dreamed about: antique structures contrasted with modern life and every single person had my favorite accent of all time. We were couch surfing, of course, but our host was a Scottish lad (*lad* feels appropriate here), and we spent the first night pub hopping, picking up his friends along the way.

I distinctly remember cramming into a cab and arriving at a posh bar with paparazzi outside and feeling severely underdressed and strikingly foreign in my silly purple-and-white fifties day dress that drew more attention to my plus-size body. This unintentional incongruity was especially glaring when compared to everyone else's slinky black and gold outfits.

As we crammed into the back of a taxi, most of us trying to figure out how to split the fare, one of the London locals we picked up along our late-night journey turned to my waifish and adventure-seeking friend, who was exuding her consistently effortless charisma, and said, "Now *that's* what an American girl should look like!"

Another passenger (nameless and faceless at this point) defended me, saying that *Hey, I was okay too,* but the original comment was still causing my head to throb from the overwhelming shame and erased anything else that was said beyond that point. The belief that I was subpar was confirmed. The belief that I wasn't enough had been named.

I felt in that moment that no matter who I was on the inside, I would forever embody the hideous aspects of America on the outside.

………

Flying as a fat person, even when the sense of adventure leaves you euphoric, is anxiety inducing. I often insist that airports should at least make the Top Ten list of "Most Stressful Places to Be," every single hub swarming with humans who are unable to walk in straight lines, are lugging all of their belongings with them, and are left in the sometimes capable, usually *not*, hands of airline companies that decide countless people's fates every day.

The horrors of flying while fat have been covered before. I'll say this though: even though I travel dozens of times a year, my traveling routine never changes. Twenty-four hours before traveling, I start to panic (usually accompanied by tears), and I stay up until I have to leave in three hours to make sure that I'm emotionally incapable of handling any sort of unexpected change that may happen while in transit.

This includes triple-checking (quadruple-checking) that everything is as streamlined as possible and my trip is as seamless as flying while fat can be. I pack everything I'll need in an emergency into a small pouch that fits in my bra, flatten my carry-on as much as I can, and then daringly tote my feels out of town.

And this is simply what happens *before* I board the tiny flying can full of other unpredictable humans who may or may not wish I had died in a car crash on the way to the airport.

But still I continue to fly, knowing full well that it's a luxury that not everyone has and one that I am immensely grateful for.

Many years have passed since that memorable night in the London cab and even though the trip left me with some residual fears about how my (now, even fatter) body might be received elsewhere, I've still had the privilege to travel to multiple countries around the world. Each of those trips creating incredible experiences I'll never forget.

It's true that my body has continued to be unwelcome in some of those countries; too large for their chairs and too imposing for the locals.[1] My body has also been welcomed in other countries; perhaps still seen as a "billboard" for the country that I reside in but inoffensive to those that I visited while there. My body is sometimes even viewed as a positive representation of a place that many newfound friends share their desire to visit or live in.

Some communities see me as a repulsive drain on the world's economy and others as the physical embodiment of financial liberty.

....

1. It's important to add here that my experiences as a fat person were and will always be minute snippets that come from someone who is only visiting for a short time. I can't imagine how frustrating and painful it must be to *live* in these places as a fat person where you are rendered both invisible and hyper visible within your own community.

I have been viewed as both an abhorrent tourist *and* an embraced visitor. I may be seen as an adversary in some areas of the world but I have also been taken in as a comrade in others. My fat (as well as white and tattooed) presence elicits countless and complex reactions, all of them unique to the place I visit. This is something that I now accept and embrace as I travel on; intent on learning from each amazing experience and knowing that one thing will likely remain the same:

I am Jes Baker. I procrastinate doing dishes with more determination than anyone else I know, believe in affirmative action also therapy as a lifestyle, am terrified of great white sharks, and have a laugh that can be heard a block away.

But when I travel, I am still one thing: America.[2]

In some places, I may be a billboard for everything that is wrong with the world, but in others I am an almighty sign promising freedom. I am a way out. I am a life raft. I am luxury in physical form.

It's interesting, isn't it? For a physical body to sometimes unintentionally represent a country that comprises over 320 million *wonderfully* diverse people?

My name is Jes Baker. I decorate amazing cakes, have lived most of my life in a hot desert without air conditioning, feel uncomfortable in wealthy settings, and will carry thirteen shopping bags on each arm because I'm the most hardcore one-tripper you will ever meet.

But if you meet me while I'm traveling, I may as well be wearing a "Hello, My Name Is" tag that reads "The Good Ol' US of A."

....

2. True story: Fat bodies are so synonymous with America in France that many of my fat Parisian pals are often approached in English by vendors under the immediate assumption that they are tourists from the US. Watching the look on the faces of merchants as they were bluntly corrected in French (highlighting their embarrassing bias) was truly priceless.

CHAPTER 19

The Bulletproof Fatty

A HALF HOUR had already passed while I stared at my screen, clicking through the same six pictures for what seemed like the seventieth time.

With every minute that passed, I absentmindedly pulled harder and harder on a fistful of hair while my sighs grew disagreeably louder. The pictures were taken by Andy, and they were all of me modeling a bikini by the side of a pool with some friends. I had initially wanted to highlight the suit in a post, but found myself unable to choose which ones to use . . . because I hated them all.

Every single one.

I was used to having a few dozen pictures to choose from[1] so I could select a handful I loved and discard the rest. And while I had been making a point to post pictures with poses that didn't fall in the "flattering" category for years, I had become spoiled by at least having some options. Sure, my body was my body, and the photos were simply a digital version of that *same* body I've always had—there was

1. That's a lie. I always made Andy take at least sixty.

nothing novel in this statement. I know this. I *also* know that there was nothing wrong with my body, that my revulsion at the images stems from a life of learning body-ideal bullshit. But no amount of logic could satisfy me that day. My brain stubbornly zeroed in on parts of my body that it seemed determined to hate: thigh rolls that were pressed together, creating a prominent and paunchy V; arms that were awkwardly positioned; and my rebelliously protruding belly, which seemed to be just *begging* for a stranger to congratulate me on my pregnancy. Even my sunglasses seemed unsightly, and I had a momentary urge to find that leopard-print suit and set it on fire. I was annoyed, feeling self-conscious, and furious about my inability to squash my illogical insecurities. I was also unwilling to let those precious few pictures go to waste.

I finally decided: *Fuck it. Fuck it all.*

I wrote about this embarrassingly fragile process, shared my hastily typed Fuck It Mantra, linked to the goddamn suit, and then clicked the Post button as violently as possible.[2] It was over. My vulnerabilities were out there for good, so I closed my laptop, and headed to Target for some post–body shame retail therapy. I was certain this was a post that most readers would skim over, and quickly move on to other more important things. At least the goddamn post was up.

I was wrong.

Instead of disappearing into the vast nothingness that usually swallows the boring things people type on the internet, it was shared and reshared. It became the most read article I'd written in months.

The comments continued for days: typed cheers for being so brave, thank-yous for continuing to inspire. The fear I had felt while writing the piece was quickly turned into something that was received by readers as absolute fearlessness. I was unbreakable, my

---

2. It's pretty impossible to release rage by trying to punish a button that only moves a fraction of a centimeter. I recommend finding other ways to cope.

Fuck It attitude lingering far longer than the moments of fragility I wrote about in detail.

This was not the first time I had experienced this 180-degree flip of a phenomenon.

Even when we find the fortitude to get vulnerable, our vulnerability as fat people is experienced and refigured as strength and invincibility. The hunger for an "invincible" role model is so deep that even when she doesn't exist, we create her from the raw materials at our disposal.

Fat people contend with plenty of stereotypes and archetypes. We're expected to play rote roles for those around us. The fat friend, a believable villain, or the nearly invisible plot device with no story of her own. The comic relief, made hilarious by our fat bodies. The nurturer, a matronly type with a soft, broad shoulder to cry on. But in the age of body positivity, one of the least examined and most insidious is what Lesley Kinzel calls "the Bulletproof Fatty."[3]

The Bulletproof Fatty doesn't care about fashion rules. She wears horizontal stripes and tight crop tops with reckless abandon. She's loud, takes up space, does everything fat people aren't supposed to do. She's the ultimate Cool Girl, cunning in her rebellion, and knows just what to say to make fat-shamers shake in their boots. She laughs at street harassers, letting their comments roll right off her back fat. The layers of leopard print combined with unshakable confidence are everything we want to see—defiance, fearlessness, the strength we crave in ourselves—all manifested for us like some neon-print fat talisman.

But the Bulletproof Fatty isn't real. When she gets home, she doubts herself. She still stares at her bingo wings some days, wishing

....

3. Because Lesley Kinzel writes about this role in terms of the women we see prominently displayed in every Yahoo Lifestyle post about the most fashionable plus-size bloggers, I also used this framework. However, this popular ideal applies to everyone who lives within a large body.

them away. She still struggles to resist diet culture. She cries after dealing with the bigotry that surrounds her daily. She hasn't thrown away the shapewear she keeps hidden in her drawers, though this is a secret for only her to know and ignore. But the expectation of her invincibility only isolates her. After all, if she has to be *invincible,* she can't be *authentic.* And if she can't be herself, what's the point?

The expectation that each of us can, and should, be a Bulletproof Fatty is harmful in the long term. Kinzel puts it better than I can:

> Making resilience against body shaming attacks an individual responsibility is self-defeating. It makes the war impossible to win. It means no one wants to hear—or to admit—the reality that being "bulletproof" means desperately fighting to accept yourself, every day, for your own survival. That's not pretty or inspiring. No one wants to understand that it means convincing yourself and reconvincing yourself that you have a right to exist in spite of a culture working very hard to tell you otherwise, and oh yes, you have a right to exist without assholes making garbage comments at you no matter how fat you are, because human dignity does not have a size limit.
>
> As humans, we crave vulnerability. It's what brings us closer together, forges the relationships that mean the most to us. But we created the Bulletproof Fatty because we can only accept vulnerability to a point. When faced with vulnerability that is too raw, too real, we push back. We apply pressure, turning its soft coal into something harder, something more cutting. Instead of seeing the vulnerability that fat people offer us, we see only armor. We make them unfuckwithable.

....

I struggled to write this chapter, leaving it until the last possible moment and seeking help from other people much smarter than I am before typing a word, not just because vulnerability is hard work, but also because I knew it would be hard for fat people to read. And as a former mental-health professional, I knew how triggering it would be for so many readers. It's tough to speak vulnerably among fat people for so many reasons.

For one, popular culture loves to imagine fat people as weak, sad, and isolated, painfully aware of our own failures. When we talk vulnerably, that stereotype echoes for us. We've been so pinned to it that loving our bodies and living lives out loud is a breath of fresh air. And it is part of our truth. But it's also not our whole truth. We deserve to own our whole truth and we can't grow if we don't.

Body-positive spaces—typically on the internet, where we're able to find others who will talk about fatness in a neutral or affirming way—have internalized the idea of the Bulletproof Fatty. We internalize this concept because many of us are traumatized by diet culture. Some of us have experienced trauma that led to us becoming fat. Others have experienced trauma as a result of living in a world that hates fat people. And almost none of us are receiving treatment for that trauma that holds space for us to *just be* as fat people.

Vulnerability is hard, made harder by trauma, and made harder still by living in a world that tells you your trauma is deserved. It's difficult to find support among fat people because so many of us carry trauma with us everywhere we go.

And when we don't work through our trauma, everything becomes a trigger. We can't talk about why we're fat. We can't talk about the trauma that led us to be fat, or the trauma of how we've been treated as fat people. We become unable to hold a conversation about the innumerable reasons that people are fat. Some people are fat because that's simply the body shape they were born into, adipose tissue playing its wonderful part in creating human diversity.

Other people are fat because of physical or mental-health complications.[4] Their body size is a symptom of something else, a visual trophy of their survival.

Regardless, none of us wants to participate in the narrative of the "depressed and traumatized fat person who eats an entire pizza when alone at night," but the reality is that sometimes I'm sad, the feelings are legitimate, and pizza saves my sanity for an evening.[5] And while I realize that this experience is *not* every fat person's experience—that many don't identify with such fat tropes at all—it is sometimes mine, and I'm okay with that.

If I were to participate in the Bulletproof Fatty narrative, I would have to pretend that I don't have a toolkit of coping mechanisms that I utilize daily to work through past and current traumas simply because some of those tools are frowned upon by others. And I refuse to do that. I am still here, still kicking ass, still reclaiming my journey, and I refuse to apologize for my hard-earned existence.

My adipose tissue, whether genetic or accumulated, is a reminder that I have been successful at surviving and that while I'm imperfect, I am still here. This is a crowning achievement, and I wouldn't turn down a medal if offered one. Just saying.

....

It took me years to realize that recovering from a lifetime of living and breathing diet culture[6] requires essentially the same process as

....
4. I'd like to make it abundantly clear that fatness is *not* a mental illness, but it can be a symptom of a mental or physical illness.

5. Feeling suicidal one day and unable to reach anyone from my support system, talk myself through, or take medication, the only thing I could manage was making pear, apple, and brie crepes from scratch. It offered a purpose, a feeling of calmness, and a delicious distraction. Crepes literally saved my life, and I feel no guilt over this. Just gratitude.

6. Also known as "That No-Fun Fatphobic Lifestyle"!

recovering from a mental illness or substance-use disorder. After working in mental health—walking others through shedding shame and learning how to live with the brain they were given—I was invested and fully believed in a culture where there was no space for negativity around this process. There was no guilt, no fault, no blame—simply the desire to move forward. I taught others how to internalize this shame-free way of living by using the Prochaska and DiClemente model for change to show that any recovery journey was complex, never linear, and would always include "relapse" as part of the healing process. Though this is a fairly accepted concept within the behavioral-health community, it is noticeably lacking in our body-image conversations.

In fellowships like Alcoholics Anonymous, the concept of each person having a sponsor—a peer you can contact when you're feeling "weak" or struggling to simply get through the day—is built into the framework. That person is there to walk you through that feeling of weakness, provide nonjudgmental support, and offer alternative ways to cope until you're able to sturdy yourself and move forward. I question why this framework seems to be missing when the issue changes from substance use to self-hatred within our body-image communities. I feel fortunate to have experienced a sort of advocacy similar to what is found in recovery programs through a few close friends, and while this small amount of support helps me immensely, I have yet to see it actively integrated within the larger fat-positive communities that we interact with online.

That very isolation, that refusal to remedy a problem we are ignoring, highlights the harm that the Bulletproof Fatty causes in our communities.

Perhaps one reason we fail to find the support we need during our "weak times" is because we, the visible body advocates, want to believe in the existence of a Bulletproof Fatty just like everyone else.

We almost feel like we *need* to find those qualities in those around us. We are so eager to know that the answer to empowerment can be found through one individual's strength alone.

The creation of the Bulletproof Fatty doesn't just lie on the shoulders of thin people. We as fat people have also perpetuated this mythical creature. We are also responsible for her viral-worthy success, and sometimes that's really hard to look at. I get it, though. I'm one of those people who still finds the Bulletproof Fatty enticing.

It's exciting to think about who we'd be if we weren't so messy, weren't so sad, weren't so flawed. We get a special kind of contact high when we find someone who seems to encapsulate impermeable qualities, but that high? It will never last. We can't just jump to the end where we "love ourselves." If we do, we miss the messiness, which is where the magic happens.[7] We don't know how to talk about the messiness, which means we don't know how to connect. And we don't know how to make space for our trauma.

It's complicated to discuss these complex issues. Even though the fight for body liberation has been around for decades, we're still learning a fairly new language that leaves a lot to be desired. Our vocabulary is still developing, and sometimes we still find ourselves at a loss when it comes to translating these theories into our own lives and conversations with each other.

This is not our fault, though it isn't getting any easier, even though "body positivity" has become an internationally recognized movement over the last few years. Corporations who promise diversity continue to market exclusivity; Weight Watchers has co-opted the message of body love; and the medical field insists on pushing

....

7. The demand for perfection in general is inextricably connected to white supremacy and colonialism. This is worth noting and it's in our best interest to stop buying it.

back against our attempts at physical reclamation, deeming obesity a disease and requiring that weight be treated first, regardless. Many professionals who work within the eating-disorder community continue to reinforce diet culture while addressing these harmful behaviors. How are we supposed to heal when those who are supposed to be helping us continue to cause harm?

It's messy, to say the least.

I don't know how we make it past the Bulletproof Fatty as a community, but I do know that we need to tend to our trauma. And when it comes to trauma, the only way through it is . . . through it.

It helps to remember that your only job is to be yourself. You just have to feel how you feel, live your own life and be your authentic self. As the wonderful poet Mary Oliver says, "You only have to let the soft animal of your body love what it loves."

I try my best to show the messiest and most real aspects of my life online, to offer authenticity and talk about the shit that makes me the most uncomfortable to balance out the days I was feelin' myself. I do what I can to offer vulnerability (while remaining safe—safety is important), and after doing this for a handful of years I have become a somewhat prominent face in many people's social media feeds.

This popularity[8]—which in part can be attributed to years spent speaking truths that made me so nervous I wanted to vomit—had also undeniably been bolstered by what others *wanted to see in me*. While constantly posting vulnerable photos (many of which were more terrifying to share than the previously mentioned bikini images), my uneasiness and internal doubt were quickly twisted into something I never intended. These pictures were greeted with *even more*

....

8. Popularity is supersubjective and feels weird to say. Let's just say that I became "well-known enough to write some books that gave me panic attacks while I typed them and then some people bought them." Fair?

enthusiasm than the ones I shared while feeling comfortable in my body. I was soon consumed by others as the fat, bitchy, tattooed superhero that people needed me to be; I became invincible, impervious to the forces of fat hate surrounding me. While fat, tattooed, and *definitely* a fantastic Super Bitch, I am in no way undefeatable. I never have been. The experience of being seen through a faulty lens of impermeability felt strange; I became cognizant of the paradoxical fact that I was both hypervisible and completely unseen. Even in my most vulnerable moments, even in those photos I honestly hated, I was transformed. My emotional nakedness, though relatable for many, was frequently reconstructed into something more palatable. I had somehow become a version of the Bulletproof Fatty.

But I am *not* a body-image superhero. No one is.

I'm not always brave. I'm not completely healed. I'm not invincible. And though I *logically* know better, I'm not always "okay" with my body.

Someone once asked me in an email: *How do you keep going when you're trying to change the way you look not only at yourself but the world? How do you not sit & cry & give up?*

My reply was honest. "I *don't* always keep going. I sometimes feel like never getting out of bed and crying all day and hating the world. Then, when all that's out of my system, I read my favorite body-positive books and hang out with people who love me. The reality is that I roar some days and sob on others."

To quote the ever brilliant Ijeoma Oluo one last time, "If somebody comes off as bulletproof, they are either lucky or lying."

None of us are the Bulletproof Fatty, because none of us are indestructible. Of course we ultimately know that, but none of us really want to act like we do. The reality is that we are beautifully, imperfectly, gorgeously, terribly human. And the goal of our work to embrace our bodies shouldn't be to be happy and confident all the time. The goal should be to allow ourselves to just *exist*.

As simple as it sounds, that's the hardest goal for many of us. Allow yourself to just exist, and work to create space for fat people to just be *people*. Messy, imperfect, kind, mean, resilient, delicate, happy, depressed, conflicted people.

It's who I am and who I will always be.

CHAPTER 20

6 Ways to Love Your Body

1) Change the word "love" to "liberate."

I've long preached the importance of *body love,* the proposed goal of falling head over heels with your physical appearance and celebrating it for how it looks regardless of how it fits (or doesn't fit) into society's definition of beauty. Body love asks you to achieve a 180-degree mental change; instead of "hating" your physical self, it insists that you can adore it for the way it looks regardless of what others may say. In theory, it's a lovely thought—worshiping your body because it's yours, because our beauty-centric culture is designed to be exclusive—to reject complete assimilation seems like the ultimate victory.

What I have come to realize, though, is that asking someone to achieve body love can quickly become another unattainable prerequisite, much like the desire to change our body into what is deemed desirable. When we focus solely on learning to "love our bodies," there is a possibility that we are simply replacing the obsessive hatred around them with an equally obsessive love.

243

And hell yeah! That's progress, right? Love is so much more desirable than hate; trading one negative emotion out for another more positive feeling is a glorious stepping stone.

But body obsession is still body obsession.

The popularity of body positivity over the last few years has morphed into something I like to refer to as Lisa Frank BoPo: a strain of rainbow-colored body empowerment, covered in sparkles, which is purposefully vague so that it ignores larger body issues like racism, ableism, and the inaccurate equation of fat equaling unhealthy. Its messaging reflects the feeling you get when remembering your Trapper Keeper, covered in adorable technicolor leopards, from elementary school. In this way, it completely ignores the reality that even though we *do* have enormous power over our thoughts and *can* change the way we view our bodies, therefore changing social norms, we still live in a world that challenges (and actively attacks) our power every single day. It takes that fact and tries to distract you with something that has "more positive vibes," not making space for daily issues that marginalized bodies face no matter how many inspirational quotes they read.

Because we live in this world, we cannot realistically escape this bigotry (which manifests itself for fat bodies in lack of health care, inaccessible cities and events, harassment, and tragically, suicide). To propose that you *absolutely can love your body, and if you don't it's because you're not trying hard enough* makes those who are affected by oppression daily feel like they're somehow failing at this movement that is allegedly supposed to offer freedom.

It's not always possible to *love* your body. And it's not something I want to ask of anyone any longer.

I have been working instead on using language that respects and acknowledges these very real barriers and find myself feeling more at home with the concept of "body liberation."

Body love comes with responsibility. It, in essence, holds you responsible for your willpower or lack thereof. It puts the onus on you to master the ability to unlearn old lies. It binds us with the opposite requirements of self-hatred, but it's still binding us. When we tell each other to *love your body* and with the implication that *if you don't, you just need to try harder,* we're not necessarily empowering anyone; we're just regurgitating logic we learned from weight loss and from diet culture.

Liberation is freedom from *all* outside expectations, even our own. Liberation is not having to love your body all the time. Liberation is not asking permission to be included in society's ideal of beauty. Liberation is bucking the concept of beauty as currency altogether. Liberation is recognizing the systemic issues that surround us and acknowledging that perhaps we're not able to fix them all on our own. Liberation is personally giving ourselves permission to live life.

Liberation is slowly learning how to become the best version of our whole selves—body included, yes. But it is no longer a requirement on our checklist of self-improvement to learn to love it.

In the end, I have found that *the less I try to force myself to love my body, the less I hate it.*

That, for me, is all I can ask for.

2) Find your support system.

You didn't learn to hate your body on your own. You don't have to learn how to liberate it on your own either. Find your people. Hug them tightly. Share your scariest secrets. Accept their compliments. Let them lift you up. Love them as hard as you can.

3) Be more like Starbucks Ken.

I've developed an overwhelming amount of gratitude for the Starbucks drive-through near my house. Its presence on the corner was sometimes the only thing strong enough to inspire me to heave myself out of bed each day while my writing deadlines loomed closer and closer; a brick-and-mortar reminder that even though *it felt* like I was going to die from early-morning sun-ray exposure[1] or the potential career suicide I was walking into by finishing this book, I probably wouldn't. If I could just drive for *seven minutes* I would be rewarded with endless shots of espresso, tomato mozzarella paninis, and, more than likely, a chipper greeting from a Starbucks employee—all of whom *never once* visibly judged my unbrushed hair or acknowledged my constant state of mania which I would try to hide (unsuccessfully) beneath my bleary smile. They also took my usual quad shot over ice with thirty-seven other specific instructions order in stride for nearly 365 days in a row.

Those baristas are literal coffee-slinging angels.

I do have a favorite barista, though, and he is basically a real-life, emphatically cheerful Ken doll who always greets me as I drive up with a "Nice to see you back, Ms. Jes!" There isn't a single trace of sarcasm in this greeting to this day. We are obviously best friends.

Ken doesn't care if my hair is obviously-just-slept-in and flattened on one side. Ken doesn't care when one eye is swollen because I sleep extra hard on my right side when I'm stressed out. Ken doesn't care that I forgot how to do laundry three months ago.

He doesn't care that my car is occasionally full of trash, and instead of giving me side-eye he'll simply state: "I like your issues of Vogue" while nodding at the stack of magazines on top of the pile of mail on my passenger seat. When I explain how ridiculous it is to get these issues every month, which I never ordered and have no interest in because *Hey* Vogue, Self, *and* Health, *your periodicals are full of poison*, Ken just laughs and says, "Well, I love looking at *GQ* but sometimes I wonder, like, where are all the dudes with 42-inch waists?"

Like I said. Best friends

....
1. I'm no vampire, but I'm also *sure as hell* not a morning person.

Aside from body image, social life, and relationship chats (my order is complicated and you can cover a lot in five minutes), Ken doesn't mind waiting. Ken doesn't even care that my order makes everything take longer; even if it's because I asked them to toast multiple blueberry muffins, and a requested last-minute change because I actually really *do* want that protein box after all. Ken doesn't care because Ken genuinely wants me to have whatever I want in life.

And so, I decided that I could take a page out of his book and just *not care* about insignificant things on which I've spent so much time waffling between "should I?" and "should I not?" and focus more on what I actually want out of my life.[2] I've decided that all of our lives would be exponentially better if we treated ourselves the way this kick-ass barista treats me.

Bless you, Ken. Bless you.

4) Get one hundred women in one room and naked in front of a camera.

A local photographer and I organized an event that came with an open invitation for any woman to join us for a nude photo shoot. Between the two, over 164 women of all shapes, sizes, shades, and ages gathered together in Tucson, Arizona, and undressed their glorious bodies for the camera and world.

Nearly everyone had something to personally gain from the experience; it was the ultimate test of self-trust. They bared all to defy a lifetime of being told that their bodies were less than camera worthy. And defy they did. Every time the shutter clicked, triumph was theirs. There were tears among the cheers.

....

2. Which is usually a complicated espresso drink and whatever muffin they recommend, but this also extends to things like only hanging out with nice people, getting a gel pedicure once a year, saying no to events that I know I'll just end up sulking at, and maintaining my HBO subscription.

The participants were and are powerhouses. Some were strong and silent powerhouses. Some were cheeky, laughing powerhouses. Some were fierce and ferocious powerhouses. And some were sobbing, shaking powerhouses . . . but they all did what *so* many are afraid to do: they exposed themselves in a light that highlighted their beautiful vulnerability. It's never easy, and every feeling imaginable arose. But they did it, and because of those images they are changing the world. Theirs, and *certainly* mine.

When you see hundreds of naked bodies (don't think these were the only naked photo shoots I've participated in) in front of you, your brain can't help but see the strength. The diversity. The absolute and undeniable beauty.

Alt option: Smash your scale.

Literally. I found myself one afternoon surrounded by dozens of women armed with their scales and their chosen tools of destruction—hammers, chainsaws, sledgehammers, baseball bats, crowbars, and, yes, even electric guitars—all of which were used to bash our collective scales[3] into a million pieces of metaphorical freedom. Some even used scales to beat other scales into submission.

The cathartic release was visible. The sounds, magnificent. The unspoken point, made.

5) Live your life as the best person you can be.

There is a lot of joy and sunshine in the world. There is also a lot of misery, fear, and, consequently, hatred. Life can be wonderful, but it can also hurt. A lot.

....

3. Pro tip learned the hard way: If your scale is primarily glass, don't smash it on gravel unless you plan on spending the rest of the night holding your cellphone flashlight above the ground and picking up shards.

I think we all look for ways to overcome that hurt. The hatred. The difficult things hurled at us whether we like it or not. While living in a fat body, figuring out how to survive harassment is something that becomes an inevitable part of your daily life.

Here is one of the most important things I can tell you: *confidence and resiliency when it comes to accepting your body has nothing to do with your body at all.*

They have everything to do with actively working toward becoming the best person you can be.[4]

When you know that you, as a full human, are a general asset to the world, what others think about your body (or about you, for that matter) seems insignificant when faced with this larger perspective. Embrace yourself as an entire person, so that no matter what happens you can go to bed at night knowing that you've done your best and that tomorrow is another day.

You are a force. A beautiful, resilient, multifaceted, force. Don't let anyone stop you . . . especially yourself.

6) Outlive the bastards.

Not outlive, like "find the fountain of youth and drink it all"; none of us are immortal, and we all will eventually die. Also, drinking from public fountains sounds super risky.

Outlive as in *live your best life out loud.* Embody happiness as much as you can. And know that sometimes this is achieved by the very simple act of imperfectly existing.

Exist in a world that doesn't want you to exist. Leave your house and engage in incredible adventures, even if others frown upon your decisions. Wear whatever you want, even when others give you restrictions. It's always a better bet to ask for forgiveness than

---

4. Some of the wisest people I know wholeheartedly cosign this as well.

permission, though I encourage you to neither wait for approval nor apologize for living your best life.

Existing really is the ultimate victory.

Sometimes it means standing on stage and preaching the truth of body liberation. Sometimes it means waking up, staying under the covers, and continuing to breathe for twenty-four hours. These are all victories, and neither is more important than another.

You deserve to exist, and I want you to find happiness and fulfillment and eventually internalize that you are not broken. The world is continually cruel, and sometimes existing within it is the greatest triumph of all. But every day that you're still here? Consider each of them a magnificent victory.

You got this, my friend.

Thank You. Thank You Very Much.

To my mom: Thank you for keeping me alive and unconditionally loved for thirty-one years, no matter how hard my brain has tried to thwart you at every turn. You are my best friend and the most incredible mother in the world.

To Andy: Thank you for letting me share all our secrets with the world, even the sex ones. I don't know many people who would be cool with that, but it's just another reason I love the eternal shit out of you. Thanks for waking me up early in the morning to write when I asked you to, even though we both know that's a potentially scarring and physically dangerous thing do given that I am consistently an ungrateful and cantankerous gargoyle when you sweetly remind me that it's time to rise and shine. Thanks for having the patience of a saint, the communication skills of a therapist, and bedroom skills that make the best porn star in the world look like an amateur. Also, thank you for coming up with the brilliant name for my next blog that will be solely about sex positivity: The Militant Spanker. You are not only a creative genius but also the love of my goddamn life.

To my grandma: Even though you sold me out when I was only eating ice cream cones for lunch in middle school, I still love you the most and always will. Love, Your Favorite Grandchild (there's no reason to deny this or roll your eyes. It's no longer a secret—everyone knows).

A nauseating and mushy thank you to Caleb Luna, Lindy West, Ijeoma Oluo, Your Fat Friend, Meghan Tonjes, Saucye West, Corissa Enneking, Alysse Dalessandro, Rachel Kacenjar, Sonya Renee Taylor, Julianne Combest, Rachel Wiley, Denise Jolly, Amy Morby, Lesley Kinzel, Kim Selling, Troy Solomon, Brittany Gibbons, Bevin Branland-ingham and every other radical human who shared their brilliance with me while I was trying to parse out the topics of this book.

Skype sucks, and the fact that you were willing to load the damn thing just to talk is a true act of love. The world is lucky to have you, and so am I. It may be a memoir, but it took a community to write.

To my therapist, Nancy: Many thanks for keeping me alive and accommodating three sessions a week when I was losing it while writing Chapter 4.

To my dad: I'm glad we're having hard conversations now. Thanks for being willing to have them with me.

Thank you to my friends, who have been continuously supportive, checking in via text with "How's the book going?" and who still continued to love me even after I began responding with nothing but poop emojis because I was incapable of stringing words together. Thanks for sticking around and not banishing me after I canceled every single hangout plan we made for months and months and . . . months.

To the rad fat babes of the internet: Thank you for inspiring me every day and reminding me that "aloneness" isn't really a thing anymore. Your existence is revolutionary and life-changing.

ABOUT THE AUTHOR

JES BAKER is a positive, progressive, and magnificently irreverent force to be reckoned with in the realm of self-love advocacy and mental health. She believes in the importance of body autonomy, hard conversations, strong coffee, and even stronger language.

After creating satirical versions of Abercrombie & Fitch advertisements in 2013, she appeared on the *Today Show* and quickly became one of the leading voices in the current body image movement.

When not writing, Jes spends her time speaking around the world, working with plus size clothing companies, organizing body liberation events, taking pictures in her underwear and attempting to convince her cats that they *like* to wear bow ties.

Learn more about Jes at TheMilitantBaker.com